THE
GREAT
AMERICAN
THINKERS
SERIES

This new series of original works is designed to present in highly readable form the flow of American thought from colonial times to the present. Each volume has been written by a leading scholar and is devoted to a single man in the history of American thought who represents a particular trend or movement within the great span of our culture. Each book in the series contains a short biography of the man, a critical evaluation of his central ideas and their influence upon American thought as a whole, as well as an extensive bibliography and an index.

The Great American Thinkers Series is designed for the general reader as well as the serious college student or higher-level secondary school student, and is under the general editorship of two distinguished American educators: Arthur W. Brown, Ph.D., President, Adelphi University; and Thomas S. Knight, Ph.D., Professor and Chairman of the Department of Philosophy, Adelphi University.

ALEXANDER HAMILTON was written by Stuart Gerry Brown, Professor of American Studies, University of Hawaii. Professor Brown, formerly of Syracuse University, is the author of THOMAS JEFFERSON in The Great American Thinkers Series.

☆

The GREAT AMERICAN THINKERS *Series*

JONATHAN EDWARDS • *Alfred Owen Aldridge*
BENJAMIN FRANKLIN • *Ralph L. Ketcham*
JOHN WOOLMAN • *Edwin H. Cady*
THOMAS JEFFERSON • *Stuart Gerry Brown*
JOHN C. CALHOUN • *Richard N. Current*
GEORGE BANCROFT • *Russel B. Nye*
CHAUNCEY WRIGHT • *Edward H. Madden*
CHARLES PEIRCE • *Thomas S. Knight*
WILLIAM JAMES • *Edward C. Moore*
THORSTEIN VEBLEN • *Douglas F. Dowd*
JOHN DEWEY • *Richard J. Bernstein*
ALEXANDER HAMILTON • *Stuart Gerry Brown*

IN PREPARATION

HENRY DAVID THOREAU • *James Murray*
JAMES MADISON • *Neal Riemer*
RALPH WALDO EMERSON • *Warren Staebler*
THEODORE PARKER • *Arthur W. Brown*
JOSIAH ROYCE • *Thomas F. Powell*
THEODORE ROOSEVELT • *William Harbaugh*
ALFRED NORTH WHITEHEAD • *Nathaniel Lawrence*
GEORGE SANTAYANA • *Willard E. Arnett*
DR. W. E. B. DU BOIS • *Henry Lee Moon*
NORMAN THOMAS • *Robert J. Alexander*

ALEXANDER HAMILTON

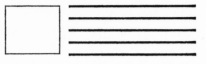

Author of this volume: Stuart Gerry Brown, Ph.D., Professor of American Studies, University of Hawaii.

Series Editors: Arthur W. Brown, Ph.D., President, Adelphi University; and Thomas S. Knight, Ph.D., Professor and Chairman of the Department of Philosophy, Adelphi University.

Twayne Publishers, Inc.   ::   New York

This Twayne Publishers edition
is published by special arrangement with
Washington Square Press, Inc.

PREFACE

To write a book about Alexander Hamilton after a lifetime of affection and admiration for Thomas Jefferson is, to say the least, an unusual experience. I have found it both invigorating and chastening: invigorating, because Hamilton was a bold and adventurous man, in and out of trouble during the whole of a very full life; chastening, because for a Jeffersonian to look at the American experiment from the point of view of Hamilton begets humility—he was so much more often right than one had always supposed!

And it is good for "democrats" to grapple once more with "aristocrats." By comparison with Hamilton's essays and speeches, even Walter Lippmann's modern classic, *The Public Philosophy,* is a weak and vacillating attempt to reassert the values of order in republican society. Students and others who wish to test the "infrastructure" of American government and of democratic political thought cannot do better than to read Alexander Hamilton. They will find his mind tough and confident, his style bold and graceful. And they may be startled to discover how relevant his ideas still may be.

I am grateful to Clinton Rossiter and Ralph Ketcham for many valuable conversations over the years; to Walter Johnson for a thoughtful reading of the final chapter; to the staff of the University of Hawaii library for courteous assistance; and to my wife for her patience and finely sharpened editorial skill.

S. G. B.

Honolulu, Hawaii
November 15, 1966

☆

CONTENTS

Preface — v

1. Revolutionary Patriot — 1

2. Lawyer and Unionist — 23

3. Secretary of the Treasury:
   The Hamilton System — 47

4. A Nation-Builder Becomes a Party-Builder — 69

5. Power Behind the Throne — 99

6. The Bitter End — 137

7. The Mind of Alexander Hamilton — 156

   Bibliographical Note — 176

   Index — 179

Chapter 1

REVOLUTIONARY PATRIOT

I

If the "father of his country" was almost universally loved and respected, it is nevertheless characteristic of many others of the founding generation of the United States that they were highly controversial men, opinionated, vigorous, often cantankerous. They were revolutionists, and it is not remarkable that revolutionists should be abrasive personalities or at best passionate partisans of contrasting philosophies. In a generation headed by Washington, the choleric John Adams and the partisan democrat Jefferson were more truly representative figures. Among them Alexander Hamilton was at home, though not in friendship, and secured his place by the brilliance of his mind and by his solid achievement as a nation-builder. If he was not, as Talleyrand put it, the greatest of the "choice and master spirits of the age," he was in any case a charismatic leader of a great faction and the authentic founder of one of the two persistent traditions of American thought. Though he was not so well hated, perhaps, as Jefferson, and certainly not so well loved, the stamp of his mind on the history of his country is no less discernible and the magnitude of his contribution worthy of comparsion with that of his bitter and irreconcilable rival. Indeed, their very irreconcilability is a principal key to understanding the American paradox of idealism and pragmatism, internationalism and isolationism, conservatism and liberalism, aristocracy and democracy. It is no small tribute to the leader of American conservatism that the great liberals from Jefferson and Madison to Franklin D. Roosevelt and John F. Kennedy have sometimes adapted his means to their ends. For his part, Jefferson would not be flattered to discover that *his* means have often been adapted to illiberal ends, and in his name. If Hamilton was always doomed to scoring partial victories only, he is still scoring them in the middle of the twentieth century: the Federal Reserve Board sets the interest rate whether the President likes it or not!

II

Unlike most of the other founders of the United States, her first great statesman-financier-politician came not from one of the thirteen colonies but from the West Indies. Hamilton was born on the island of Nevis, the illegitimate son of James Hamilton, a Scottish businessman who was moving about the British West Indies from one failing venture to another, and Rachel Fawcett Lavien, who left her German businessman husband to live with Hamilton. We know little about the elder Hamilton, except that he was an attractive man whose optimism seems to have condemned him always to overestimate his prospects. Alexander, as a man, often asserted that his father's blood was "as good as that of those who plume themselves upon their ancestry." And from time to time the younger Hamilton sent money to his father. Rachel Lavien was a dark beauty from whom Hamilton may have inherited something of his characteristic spirit and charm.

Hamilton's youth remains obscure despite intensive research. It is now settled that he was born in 1755, two years earlier than had long been supposed, so that he was rather less of a prodigy than either he or his contemporaries thought he was. But little is known of his boyhood except that he lived in St. Croix, that he was apprenticed as clerk to the firm of Nicholas Cruger in 1766 at the age of eleven, that his mother died two years later, and that he showed genuine precocity as a writer and accountant.

In September, 1772, when he was seventeen, Hamilton impressed his elders with his skill as a writer by making a kind of prose poem out of his experience during a severe Caribbean hurricane. In the form of a letter to the *Royal Danish American Gazette,* the young author not only gave a vivid description of the event itself but worked up a long apostrophe to show how the experience affected him:

> Where now, oh vile worm! is all thy boasted fortitude and resolution? What is become of thine arrogance and self-sufficiency? Why dost thou tremble and stand aghast? How humble, helpless, how contemptible you now appear. And for why? The jarring of elements—the discord of clouds? Oh! impotent presumptuous fool! how durst thou offend that Omnipotence, whose nod alone were sufficient to quell the destruction that hovers over thee, or crush thee into atoms? etc., etc.

If such writing sounds stilted, even bombastic, to modern ears, it should be remembered that Hamilton's style was formed under the conventions of the eighteenth century. Judged in appropriate terms, there was reason to suppose that the author of the "Hurricane Letter" might grow into an important man of letters.

At any rate, it was as a poet and essayist that young Hamilton first came to public notice. A month later, with the help of Hugh Knox, a Presbyterian minister, Cruger and other friends, enough money was raised to send him off to New York to get a college education. The diligent young clerk gave promise of becoming a leading citizen of his native islands. He planned to study medicine and was expected to return and practice in St. Croix. As it turned out, he did study medicine for a short time, but he never returned to the islands. His mentors, nevertheless, had before long good reason to boast of their decision to back him.

III

Hamilton arrived in New York in the fall of 1772, hoping to enter King's College (Columbia). But his preparation was inadequate, owing to the sketchy nature of his studies in St. Croix, and a year of pre-college study was recommended. Settling at Elizabethtown, New Jersey, he enrolled at Dr. Barber's preparatory school, applied himself with a diligence which had already become habitual, and after completing his course, applied for admission to the College of New Jersey (Princeton). However, when President Witherspoon turned down his appeal to be allowed to accelerate his program, Hamilton returned to New York in the fall of 1773 and enrolled as a special student at King's College. Here he continued his studies until the outbreak of the Revolution. But though he improved his knowledge of the Greek and Roman classics, absorbed as much science as was available in the curriculum and read deeply in modern history, his mind was more and more engaged by the developing struggle between England and her colonies.

The students at Columbia were divided by temperament and by growing conviction into loyalists and rebels. Hamilton, the future arch apostle of conservatism and tradition, was a natural and effective rebel. Indeed, it is instructive to compare his early writing and speeches with those that were flowing from the pen of Thomas Jefferson at the same time. Differences of opinion and theory were slight, similarities to be found everywhere. While still only nineteen, Hamilton entered the pamphlet wars with a vigorous defense of the Boston tea dumpers. "Perhaps," he wrote, "before long your tables and chairs, and platters, and dishes, and knives, and forks, and everything else, would be taxed. Nay, I don't know but they would find means to tax you for every child you got, and for every kiss your daughters received from their sweethearts; and God knows, that would soon ruin you!" Broad humor of this sort became a characteristic of Hamilton's lifelong pamphleteering, as did the cutting and the acid.

In an exchange with the Tory clergyman Samuel Seabury, Hamilton began to make use of the Lockean doctrine of the social contract which guided most of the American revolutionaries, notably Jefferson. The right of rebellion inhered, the young rebel argued, in any body politic which was abused by its sovereign, since the status of the sovereign rested upon the will of the body politic. However, Hamilton had no wish to break the bonds of empire. If only the British could see the unlimited economic potential in a wise policy of cooperation with the American colonies, a commonwealth of riches and happiness beyond the dreams of men could readily come into being. This was the most desirable solution to the tensions then building up. But if the British persisted in their blindness, exacting tribute in the form of taxes and prescribing crippling rules for American commerce, there would be a parting of the ways. In an economic struggle, the Americans, Hamilton maintained, had the advantage and would surely triumph. If, at the worst, war should break out, the Americans in the end would surely win. At any rate, the cause of the Americans was no more and no less than the rights of free-born Englishmen, seeking justice under the British constitution. The King and Parliament were violating the organic law of the empire; it was the duty of honest men to protest by whatever means would be effective. "The sacred rights of mankind," he wrote, "are not to be rummaged for among old parchments or musty records. They are written as with a sunbeam in the whole volume of human nature, by the hand of divinity itself, and can never be erased or obscured by mortal power." The florid style perhaps displays the author's youthful enthusiasm more than the fine point of doctrine, but in essentials what he was saying was identical with what Jefferson was then setting forth in his first famous pamphlet, *A Summary View of the Rights of British America.* And Tom Paine himself, afterward anathema to Hamilton, could hardly have uttered a more fervent conviction of the rights of man.

As the issues were drawn ever more sharply in 1774–75, Hamilton joined the New York militia and began to think in terms of an inevitable military conflict. In the coming war he saw an opportunity not only to serve his adopted country but to advance himself in its councils. He was to serve with passion and with devotion, but his talents for administration and management generally conspired to defeat his hopes of glory on the field of battle—both in the Revolution and afterward, when he aspired to command the United States Army.

Hamilton first came under fire in a skirmish in New York City on August 23, 1775, when he helped rescue some cannon on the Battery under the guns of a British man-of-war. Except for a few months in 1781, he was thereafter continuously in active military service until the battle of Yorktown brought an end to the hostilities. In March, 1776, he was given command of an artillery company and during that year fought in the battles of Long Island, Harlem Heights, White Plains and Trenton. It was at Harlem that he is supposed to have had his first meeting with Washington. There are no records of such a fateful encounter, but there is no doubt that the older man soon enough saw that Hamilton combined to an unusual degree personal charm and qualities of leadership with ability, persistence and courage. Not long after the battle of Princeton, in the early spring of 1777, Washington invited Hamilton to join his "family" as aide-de-camp with the rank of lieutenant colonel. Thus began an alliance which played the central role not only in organizing the colonial troops into an army that could win the war but in the still more demanding task of constructing a nation out of the disparate elements the Revolution itself could scarcely hold together.

IV

In after years, to have been with Washington at Valley Forge—indeed, to have been on his staff at all—was as certain to bring political advancement as anything could be in politics. Among others, John Marshall, Aaron Burr and James Monroe profited for years by their wartime assignments with Washington. But none was so close to Washington as Alexander Hamilton or so continuously by his side. Almost from the beginning of their association the older man found that he could rely upon the younger not only to do what needed to be done, if it could be done, but to anticipate the needs. Hamilton served as secretary, administrative assistant, speech writer, and in personal terms as a kind of surrogate for the son Washington was never to have. No one could ever accuse Washington of giving special privileges to a favorite; but there was certainly a quality of affection in his relation with Hamilton which set it apart from his more formal dealings with other members of his staff.

Hamilton, for his part, gave full measure of loyalty and service to his chief, and took every honorable advantage he could of the opportunities afforded him by the association to make such valuable friends and acquaintances as Lafayette, Philip Schuyler and Henry Knox.

In 1777, Hamilton had the first of many dramatic opportunities to demonstrate his loyalty. Washington sent him to General Horatio Gates, recent victor at Saratoga, with orders to post detachments of his armies south to help with the campaign in eastern Pennsylvania. Gates balked, pleading the need to reinforce New England—which he could do without moving his encampments. Hamilton persisted, reported heatedly to Washington, and informed both Congress and the New York legislature that Washington was Commander in Chief and could only command if his generals were cooperative. In the end, with the intervention of Governor George Clinton of New York, Hamilton managed to detach some of Gates's troops and personally saw them to their new assignment.

Not long afterward, in the "Conway cabal" to oust Washington, Hamilton was again not only loyal but effective. His reports kept his chief accurately informed, and his emphatic messages to the rebellious officers reminded them of the dangers of politics under enemy guns. Thereafter, for the duration of the war, no one seriously questioned Washington's leadership. Hamilton, like the "man in the street," simply identified Washington with the Revolution itself. "All the true and sensible friends of their country," he wrote to a friend, "ought to be upon the watch to counterplot the secret machinations of his enemies."

Service on the staff of the Commander in Chief was frequently too sedentary an occupation for Hamilton. He continually begged Washington to give him a field command so that he could engage the enemy personally. Washington appreciated the young man's hot-blooded patriotism, but needed him alive too much to risk his death in battle. Upon occasion, however, circumstances conspired to give Hamilton a sudden opportunity for glory. At Monmouth, for example, the main Continental Army caught up with the advance force of General Charles Lee, who had refused to make a stand against the British. When Washington personally ordered a stand to be made, Hamilton impudently rode up to Lee, calling out, "I will stay here with you, my dear General, and die with you: let us all die here rather than retreat!" Lee declined the invitation, explaining to Hamilton that a general's duty was to his men. But Hamilton charged again and again, eventually having his horse shot from under him, until the British abandoned the field—defeated by a combination of rebels, heat and mosquitoes.

After Monmouth, Washington proposed to cite Hamilton for gallantry, in his dispatches to Congress. With a show of modesty he regretted in later years when a Congressional citation would have been politically useful, Hamilton asked that the paragraph be omitted. But he was not willing to let Lee get off without punishment for what he was convinced was cowardice in the face of the enemy. Hamilton spoke so sharply against Lee's conduct that the General demanded a court-martial. At the trial Hamilton and another Washington aide, John Laurens, testified so harshly that Lee was convicted and suspended from command for a year. In a pamphlet defense, Lee wrote so disparagingly of Washington that several of the Commander-in-Chief's friends challenged him to duel. In the end Laurens and Lee actually fought, with Hamilton as Laurens' second. No one was seriously injured, and Lee apologized. But the enduring consequence of the whole episode was that it tied Hamilton even closer to Washington, and permanently identified the two men in the public mind.

v

Hamilton's political education was not interrupted by the war. At the request of his New York friends, he wrote regularly to the legislature at Albany to provide firsthand accounts of the progress of the war and to give the legislators detailed information on matters of military logistics and administration. This semiformal correspondence helped to establish Hamilton as a public man. And he lost no useful occasion to comment on affairs of the nation as well as the state.

His criticism of the Continental Congress was shrewd and caustic. The largely impotent Congress was a source of constant frustration to most soldiers and their officers, but to none more than Colonel Hamilton as he struggled to manage the

Continental line on behalf of the Commander in Chief. The chaotic system of correspondence with the Quartermaster General's office, various committees of Congress, state governors and state militia officials impressed upon the young Hamilton the urgent necessity of a strong, authoritative central government if the nation was to survive its infancy. A member of Congress he could honor as "a founder of an empire," but the system he deplored. In view of Hamilton's later leanings toward monarchial forms, and his distrust of democracy and liberalism, it is important to notice that already in his youth he was looking for an agency of government capable of more efficient use of power than a representative assembly, and that his search was inspired by the facts of revolutionary life, not by prior doctrine or prejudice.

Hamilton's contempt for Congressional inefficiency was so poorly concealed that he found himself, in the spring of 1779, the object of a vicious whispering campaign labeling him as a conspirator to set up a military dictatorship. The source of the story has never been certainly discovered. But there is good reason to believe that those who spread it were partisans of Lee or Gates or, at the least, among the detractors of Washington who rightly identified Hamilton as the right hand of the Commander in Chief. To hurt Hamilton by such a story was to hurt Washington himself.

At any rate, Hamilton was accused of saying in public that "it was high time for the people to rise, join General Washington, and turn Congress out of doors." Washington himself apparently counseled his aide to ignore the matter, but Hamilton saw not only serious damage to Washington in such whispers but the possible destruction of his own career. He determined to run it down. The story was first traced to Congressman Francis Dana of Massachusetts, who had repeated it as having been overheard in a tavern where Hamilton was fulminating against Congress. Hamilton went directly to Dana, demanding either his authority or an apology. He got both. The authority, it turned out, was a Massachusetts minister named William Gordon; as for Dana, he wrote "as Col. Hamilton will know the authority upon which I mentioned the declaration, so I presume he will be satisfied I did not fabricate it, as I am, from his denial of it, that he never made it." Dana out of the way, Hamilton went after Gordon, but got only evasive and condescending replies. If Gordon had not been a clergyman, Hamilton would certainly have challenged him to a duel. Instead he accused him flatly of being unable to reveal the source of his story because he had invented it. ". . . I am well informed you have established a character which in the opinion of every man of sense has forfeited all title to the delicacy of treatment usually attached to your function. I only lament that respect to myself obliges me to confine the expression of my contempt to words."

Gordon, at this point, played his trump card. Having offered repeatedly to "lay the whole matter before Congress," he now, instead, laid it before Washington. The intent to destroy Hamilton was clear enough. Americans who, now as then, deplore the practice of anonymous informing and character assassination may still take a certain satisfaction from the fact that it was Gordon, not Hamilton, who was demeaned by the transaction. Washington simply told Gordon that he could give no credence to such tales; that he would not concern himself with them; that if there were serious charges to be made they should be made in public with sworn witnesses, etc. As for the Commander in Chief, he was too busy with the war to be worried lest his most trusted and loyal aide were secretly trying to undo all that together they were trying to do. That ended the matter. It was the first, but not the last time that Hamilton was to suffer from the attacks of would-be character assassins. His sharply expressed opinions often offended people less toughened to the give and take of political battle than he was; his position close to Washington, or at the center of government, or at the head of a political party, often made him a prime object both of envy and of hopes for favors. If it was not, perhaps, an irrevocable destiny, it was certainly something in his character and temper that moved Alexander Hamilton from his clash with the busybody Gordon through a quarter-century of controversy and polemic toward tragedy on the heights at Weehawken.

But between bouts of political controversy and battles, both military and administrative, Hamilton found time during the war years to read and to reflect on government. His almost daily experience with the failures of the Confederation led him not so much to despair of the future of his country as to try to think through what could be done to make it succeed. Seven years before the Constitutional Convention, the young revolutionary soldier was grappling with the fundamental ideas which grew ultimately into the system of government he strove to put into being in the 1790s and which his country, in one guise or another, largely adopted.

In a remarkable letter to his friend James Duane (September 3, 1780) Hamilton discoursed at length and in detail both on what he thought were the weaknesses of the Confederation and what he then thought could and should be done about them. At the root of the problem was the divided sovereignty. "The idea of an uncontrollable sovereignty in each state," he wrote, "will defeat the other powers given to Congress." He cited the experience of other federations, much as James Madison was to do in later years, to show that divided sovereignty leaves the central organ of government subject to partial, intermittent or even continuous paralysis. The states could frustrate Congress' conduct of the war at any moment that a state governor or legislature believed that the interest of the state called for a disposition of its economic or military forces different from that planned and commanded by Washington on behalf of the whole nation. While state governors, as commanders of the militia, generally sought to cooperate with the Continental line under Washington, they were not obliged to do so, and Congress had no power to compel performance of any action by any state. Taxes could not be levied; Congress could only pass bills calling upon the states for contributions and urging the thirteen separate sovereignties to comply. So it had been in Greece before Athenian hegemony was established; so it had been with the Swiss cantons. So, thought Hamilton, it would always be without a strong effective sovereign over the whole territory and people to be governed.

Congress itself, even within the drastically limited powers it could exercise, was inefficient and desultory because of its administrative methods. To direct foreign affairs or military procurement by committee was to make of every decision a political issue to be resolved only by negotiation. Since the committee members were themselves the agents of their states, they took their committee positions as opportunities to continue the watch over what was thought to be the special interest of the states. Thus not only was the Congress itself a kind of continuously sitting treaty organization, but the committees preserved the principal weaknesses of the system intact. Hamilton's remedy for this defect was simply to appoint individuals to each of the administrative tasks, give them power to act on behalf of Congress and make them responsible to that body for their conduct. He would, in short, establish a kind of ministry on the British model, in which a department head had effective authority to run his department subject only to censure or recall by the legislative body. "A question has been made," he wrote, "whether single men could be found to undertake these offices. I think they could, because there would be then everything to excite the ambition of candidates. But in order to do this Congress by their manner of appointing them and the line of duty marked out must show that they are in earnest in making these offices, offices of real trust and importance." Here was at least a tentative statement of what was to become the key to the whole Hamiltonian system—the ambition and self-interest of men.

Thus in his middle twenties and in the midst of war Hamilton sketched out the main lines of his constitutional system: one authoritative central body with power to compel the states and with direct taxing and police powers over the citizens; an administrative system headed by ministers with clear lines of authority from the central legislature; the whole cemented by the self-interest of the participants—the states concerted by their need to win the war and to secure the peace; the people by their power to recall their servants; the administrators by their desire to wield power. In later years Hamilton was to decide that economic self-interest was a necessary ingredient, that money did indeed speak louder than words. But his famous appeals to the rich to protect their holdings and to the ambitious to increase theirs only filled up the forms he was articulating in these early suggestions to a legislator friend in New York.

During the same period Hamilton also anticipated, remarkably, his later views on the specific subject of public finance. In the "off season" at Valley Forge and elsewhere, he read all the books he could find on economics and fiscal management and thus acquired a knowledge of the theory of money unusual at that time in America. In a significant letter to Philip Schuyler, his future father-in-law, he tried out his ideas on how to shore up the finances of Congress. While he advocated a revaluation of the dollar which would have been confiscatory and which he would certainly not have approved in later years, he proposed to maintain the soundness of his devaluated money by establishing a central bank. This bank, to be known as the Bank of the United States, would be capitalized at $200 million, with half of the stock privately subscribed and half owned by the government. Direction would be in the hands of the private investors but government would have a voice through a minority of government-appointed directors. The whole scheme is strikingly similar to the bank he in fact established when he was Secretary of the Treasury ten years later. A year after the letter to Schuyler (1781), he set forth similar suggestions in a letter to Robert Morris, who had just been appointed to reorganize the finances of the country. Morris, indeed, tried without success to put a plan similar to Hamilton's into effect.

VII

War, administration and political speculation still did not entirely occupy Alexander Hamilton's mind. He was as devoted to pleasure and to the company of ladies as any other young officer—perhaps a bit more! He was also developing, as early as 1779, a serious interest in marriage, both because he wanted steady and attractive female companionship, and because he knew that a good marriage would be an indispensable asset in his efforts to reach the top of society and power in the country he was helping to identify and establish. A somewhat tongue-in-cheek letter to his intimate friend Laurens (April, 1779) not only reveals what he was looking for in a wife, but suggests something of the cast of his mind and spirit at that time.

Such a wife as I want [he wrote] will be difficult to be found. . . . Take her description—She must be young, handsome (I lay most stress upon a good shape) sensible (a little learning will do) well bred (but she must have an aversion to the word ton) chaste and tender (I am an enthusiast in my notions of fidelity and fondness) of some good nature, a great deal of generosity (she must neither love money nor scolding, for I dislike equally a termagent and an economist). In politics, I am indifferent what side she may be of; I think I have arguments that will easily convert her to mine. As to religion a moderate stock will satisfy me. She must believe in god and hate a saint. But as to fortune, the larger stock of that the better. You know my temper and circumstances and will therefore pay special attention to this article in the treaty. Though I run no risk of going to Purgatory for my avarice; yet as money is an essential ingredient to happiness in this world—as I have not much of my own and as I am very little calculated to get more either by my address or industry; it must needs be, that my wife, if I get one, bring at least a sufficiency to administer to her own extravagances. You will be pleased to recollect in your negotiations that I have no invincible antipathy to the *maidenly beauties* and that I am willing to take the *trouble* of them upon myself.

Laurens did not find a wife for Hamilton, even if he took the mission seriously. But by the end of 1780 Hamilton had found one for himself. His courtship and marriage to Betsy Schuyler have always held a favored place in the history of American romance, as they did in the public life of their time. When Betsy's beauty and family standing are matched to

Hamilton's charm and talent, it is not hard to understand why.

As a lover, Hamilton's literary talent served him well. The style of an eighteenth-century courtship does not wholly obscure it even today. This, for example:

> I would not have you imagine Miss that I write to you so often either to gratify your wishes or to please your vanity; but merely to indulge myself and to comply with that restless propensity of my mind, which will not allow me to be happy when I am not doing something in which you are concerned. This may seem a very idle disposition in a philosopher and a soldier; but I can plead illustrious examples in my justification. Achilles had liked to have sacrificed Greece and his glory to his passion for a female captive; and Anthony lost the world for a woman. I am sorry the times are so changed as to oblige me to summon antiquity for my apology, but I confess, to the disgrace of the present age, that I have not been able to find many who are as far gone as myself in such laudable zeal for the fair sex.

Or this:

> How happy am I to think that one month puts an end to our long separation; shall I find you my Dear girl as impatient to receive me as I shall be to fly to your bosom? I have ever since you gave me leave to do it, considered loved and cherished you as my own; but the prospect of your being so by those sacred ties which society has established and heaven approves has something delightful in it, that I find myself incapable of expressing. How often have I with *Eloisa* exclaimed against those forms which I now revere as calculated to knit our union together by new and stronger bands. It is not true that—
>
> > Love free as air at sight of human ties
> > Spreads his light wings and in a moment flies.

A sincere passion takes pleasure in multiplying the ties by which it is held to its object, and every new sanction is a new gratification.

On December 14, 1780, Alexander Hamilton married Elizabeth Schuyler, and thereby contracted not one but several of the most important relationships of his life. As the son-in-law of General Philip Schuyler, he was free and welcome to move in the best of the New York society of that day. His father-in-law was a man of great wealth and great reputation both as a soldier and as a public man. Unlike such Southern gentlemen as Jefferson, Madison or Edmund Randolph, Schuyler was untouched by democratic sentiment and un-moved by the liberal philosophy of the Enlightenment. He was a Revolutionary patriot but no revolutionary. Hamilton and Schuyler were nearly as well matched in political disposition as were Hamilton and Betsy in charm and good looks. And Schuyler's money and influence soon turned out to be among Hamilton's most useful political instruments.

He also acquired a celebrated sister-in-law, Angelica Schuy-ler Church, a great beauty and a cosmopolitan hostess. In London, Paris, New York and later in Philadelphia, her talents brought together the most interesting available company. It was Angelica Church who provided the only personal link between Hamilton and Jefferson. In the 1780s, when he was American Minister at Paris, Jefferson was an intimate of Angelica's circle and she held firm to his friendship in after years, even when the most bitter political differences had arisen between Jefferson and her family. Her warm and endur-ing friendship for her brother-in-law was equally unpolitical. In fact, at times its quality was so warm as to excite the sort of gossip that always trailed Hamilton in and out of the drawing rooms of state and of society. But such gossip was only malicious.

Despite his miserable affair with Mrs. Reynolds—at the very height of his political power—there is no reason to doubt that Hamilton's preference for Betsy above all other women was steady and sure. What is equally certain is that no public man could have had a more charming partner to rear his children and grace his table. Betsy Hamilton stood by her husband in every crisis of his crisis-filled life, and no word critical of her manner or conduct has survived—no doubt because none was ever recorded.

VIII

But Betsy Hamilton's modest and gentle disposition was in sharp contrast to her husband's. Frustrated by Washington's repeated refusals to give him a field command and, perhaps, filled with too great a sense of his own importance as he contemplated the power and prestige of his staff post and the distinction of his marriage, Alexander Hamilton was, as the saying went even at that day, "riding for a fall." It was no small irony that his hotheaded break with Washington should have come as a consequence of his admirable conduct in the Arnold affair.

In September, 1780, while returning with Washington from conferences at Hartford, Connecticut, with French General Rochambeau, Hamilton went on ahead of his chief to stop at West Point, where Benedict Arnold was in command. As he was sitting with the General, an orderly brought information that Major John André, aide to British General Sir Henry Clinton, had been captured behind American lines in civilian clothes and that incriminating documents had been removed from his person. At this juncture General Arnold excused himself, telling Hamilton that he would return presently. Instead, he sneaked out of the building, took a path through the woods to the river and got safely aboard the British warship *Venture*. When the sensational defection was discovered, Hamilton went hastily in pursuit. He was, of course, too late and could only report the disaster to Washington when the latter arrived at West Point.

Arnold had left his wife, the beautiful and ambitious Peggy Shippen of Philadelphia, to protect herself as best she could. Her best, it turned out, was very good indeed. She received Washington and Hamilton with a piece of acting well suited to her predicament. She was in bed, décolleté, overcome with shock and various kinds of emotion. The Commander in Chief and the young colonel were overwhelmed with pity and concern. As for Hamilton, he was also overwhelmed by the gentlemanly impression made by Major André. This polished and courageous man, he thought, ought not to suffer hanging as a spy while the perfidious Arnold, who had deserted both his wife and his country, got off without a scratch. Hamilton finally wrote to Sir Henry Clinton, without permission, proposing a trade of André for Arnold. Clinton refused to sanction the exchange and André, to Hamilton's growing admiration, refused to submit himself to it. Thereafter Hamilton could do nothing except try to get Washington to suspend the rules of war and allow André to die as an officer before a firing squad instead of as a spy on the gallows. Washington refused flatly, insisting that such an indulgence would undermine the whole structure of the military code. Hamilton was furious and permitted his disgust to be known. For the first time, and with unhappy consequences for both men, Hamilton spoke publicly in disparaging terms of the character of his chief.

Not long after his marriage, Hamilton reached a point of inner tension he could not control, and precipitated an open break with Washington that was perhaps inevitable after the Arnold affair. In February, 1781, at the headquarters in Morristown, Washington and his staff were deeply involved in reaching a decision as to whether to attempt the liberation of New York City or to move to the Chesapeake and endeavor to bring an end to the successes of Cornwallis. Enlistments were lagging, however, and there were mutinous elements among the troops. It was, in fact, the moment of deepest crisis in the whole war. Under these circumstances, Hamilton was stopped by Washington one morning as he descended the stairs and asked to step into his room. Hamilton replied that he would do so as soon as he had delivered a letter. But before returning he fell in with Lafayette and conversed for several minutes. When he reached the head of the stairs before Washington's room, he was met by the Commander in Chief in a towering rage. "Colonel Hamilton," he shouted, "you have kept me waiting at the head of the stairs these ten minutes. I must tell you, sir, you treat me with disrespect." Hamilton replied, hotly and instantly, "I am not conscious of it, sir, but since you have thought it necessary to tell me so, we part." Washington, of course, was taken aback, but remembering no doubt that anger too readily begets anger, he answered quietly, "Very well, sir, if it be your choice."

This small but significant episode permanently altered the relationship between the two men, and decisively affected the character of Alexander Hamilton. Perhaps his unruly spirit would never have come under effective discipline anyway. But it is certain that his haughty and irascible manner of dealing with this incident became his characteristic manner of treating anyone who crossed him afterward. It is difficult to reconcile Hamilton's handling of the matter with his immense talent, or with his equally immense ambition. That, in effect, he "got away with it" was owing solely to the stern self-discipline and the unfailing good manners of Washington.

What Hamilton did was to recount the episode to Lafayette, in disparagement of Washington, and write a self-righteous letter to his father-in-law. As one reads this letter, now available in the original manuscript showing how carefully Hamilton worked over it, it is well to remember that he was still a young man. At twenty-six he had seen more of the world and had a broader experience and held greater responsibilities than had most Americans of his age. Yet others of the founding generation in America had managed to mature beyond Hamilton while still in their twenties. The studious Madison, for example, at twenty-six had already formulated the bold new doctrine of religious freedom which was one of the chief contributions of the American Revolution to the growth of modern democracy and liberty, and had, at the same time, earned a reputation for discipline and decorum in his personal conduct. Edmund Randolph, also dear to Washington, at the same age had already helped to write the constitution of Virginia, served in the Congress and been for several years attorney general of his state, while impressing his elders and contemporaries as a man of cool judgment and disciplined behavior. And Hamilton's colleague, sober-sided James Monroe, had already left the army to become a member of the Virginia wartime Council of State. If Hamilton was not wholly set off from such men by the wealth of his charm and talent, he certainly was by the magnitude of his opinion of himself, unconsciously revealed in the letter to Schuyler.

After giving his father-in-law a careful account of the incident which led to his break with Washington, Hamilton boastfully recounts how, "in less than an hour" one of the General's aides was "assuring me of Washington's great confidence in my abilities, integrity, usefulness and of his desire in a candid conversation to heal a difference which could not have happened but in a moment of passion." Wholly blind to the generosity Washington was thus showing to the younger man, Hamilton goes on, "I requested Mr. Tilghman to tell him that I had taken my resolution in a manner not to be revoked." He would, he said, agree to the interview if the matter were pressed, but he begged to be excused. On the other hand, he told Schuyler, he did not "wish to distress Washington or the public business, by quitting him before he could derive other assistance by the return of some of the Gentlemen who were absent." In short, he would not walk out until someone came to take his place!

What follows is even more interesting and revealing of Hamilton's character and temper. He assures Schuyler that he was not "precipitate in rejecting the overture made by the General." On the contrary, he was acting on "maxims I had long formed for the government of my own conduct." It turned out that he not only hated his job as aide-de-camp but had only agreed to take it because of "the enthusiasm of the times." He had had "an idea of the General's character which," he said, "experience" soon taught him to be "unfounded." Indeed, "for three years past," he told Schuyler, "I have felt no friendship for him and have professed none." That Washington had been given no inkling of this coldness, Hamilton does not observe.

What he does go on to say is that because Washington's "competitors have slender abilities and less integrity . . . his popularity has often been essential to the safety of America, and is still of great importance to it." It was "these considerations," Hamilton pompously notes, that "have influenced my past conduct respecting him, and will influence my future."

He meant, of course, to say his "future conduct toward Washington," but the blunt and incomplete sentence was full of prophecy. There is no reason to doubt Hamilton's sincerity when he goes on to tell Schuyler he thinks it "necessary he [Washington] should be supported." In all the years afterward he certainly held the same view and with the same sincerity. Yet the element of using Washington, not only for the public good but for Hamilton's private ambition, was always central in Hamilton's perspective, from these early moments until the final months of Washington's life in 1799, when, as Inspector General of the Army, Hamilton served him for the last time.

As for the quarrel itself, Washington's decency prevented Hamilton from making as great a fool of himself as he might otherwise have done. Though he told Schuyler it was "the policy of both sides" to "conceal and cover the separation with some plausible pretext" and that the whole matter was to be kept "in confidence," it was Washington who held his counsel and Hamilton who told the story behind the General's back, to the bewilderment but continuing silence of the latter.

Hamilton stayed on with Washington for two months, but on April 30 he resigned formally, once more imploring Washington—somewhat inconsistently—to reward him for his meritorious service with a command in the line. At this point Washington leaned as far backward as he could to placate Hamilton, made him Lieutenant Colonel of light infantry and asked him to be patient until a command could be obtained. Hamilton went home, chafing at the delays which kept him from the field of glory. But on July 31, 1781, at Dobbs Ferry, New York, the long-awaited opportunity finally became a reality. Hamilton took command of a new brigade of light infantry and went off to war.

If his behavior was pompous at times and overbearing at others, it never lacked vigor or courage. And though the same imp which had led him years before to bait General Charles Lee led him now to plague Lafayette, under whom he served, to grant him favors and honors at the expense of others longer in the line, the favors and honors had all to do with winning battles and getting on with the war. And so it came about that the long years of frustrated desk work and subordination to men whose abilities he derided were rewarded with a hero's role at Yorktown. In the end, on the fourteenth of October, it was Lieutenant Colonel Alexander Hamilton of the New York Infantry who personally commanded the first charge, personally stormed and took the first redoubt, and opened the way for the main army under Washington and the French under Vumenal and Rochambeau to apply the fatal clamp that led to Cornwallis' surrender and secured independence for the new United States of America.

Chapter 2

LAWYER AND UNIONIST

I

The war over, Alexander Hamilton returned to New York to adjust himself as well as he could to private and domestic life. He was just twenty-seven. His rich experience in the field of administration had prepared him for public service, and the acquaintance he had formed with public men throughout the country, as well as the responsibilities of power, had given him a taste for action on what was called "the public stage." In the fashion of the time, he pretended to deny it. "I lose all my taste for the pursuits of ambition," he wrote a friend, "I sigh for nothing but the company of my wife and baby." (The first of his eight children, Philip, had been born January 22, 1782.) But in taking up the study of law in the office of his older friend, Colonel Robert Troup, he was conscious of both the money to be made at the bar and the usefulness of legal training for a career in government.

His return to public life began in May, when he was appointed by Congress to be Receiver of Taxes for New York. In early July he completed his reading of the law and was admitted to the bar at Albany. Almost before he had begun to practice, he was thrusting himself forward into political life by memorializing the New York legislature, urging that body to join in a call for a national convention to revise the Articles of Confederation. The legislature not only enacted his resolution, but presently elected him delegate to Congress.

And so, scarcely six months after he had returned to private life, Hamilton set off for Philadelphia and a public career that was to continue, in one office or another, for thirteen years and, whether in or out of office, to end only with his tragic death twenty-two years later.

In the Congress, Alexander Hamilton soon found himself working most closely with Robert Morris, the Superintendent of Finance, and James Madison of Virginia, whom Hamilton now met for the first time. In the struggle to shore up the finances of the new republic, these three became a triumvirate. When that effort failed and Morris was almost forcibly retired from public life, Hamilton and Madison continued to work together to build and secure a government that would make of the thirteen states and their confederation assembly a genuine nation. The New Yorker and the Virginian collaborated so effectively that they have no peers among the "Founding Fathers," yet their eventual rupture and partisan affiliation was·implicit from the beginning. What brought Madison and Hamilton together was their patriotism, their determination that the new nation which had been born in such agony should not stifle for lack of breath before it could grow up. What divided them was their different perspectives on the nature of man, on liberty and on republican democracy. At the crucial early stage they could and did sublimate these differences by their devotion to the business of making and getting adopted a national constitution. But once in operation, it became a question of what policy the new government should adopt. Then their differences quickly came to the surface and forced the two men ever farther apart. The consequence was a major part of the political warfare that shook the country for a decade. The eventual and final victory of Madison and his "great collaborator," Jefferson, was nevertheless full of ironies. It was, for example, President Madison who signed into law the re-charter of Hamilton's hated Bank of the United States, twelve years after Hamilton's death. But in Philadelphia in 1782 there were no ironies in the political relations of these two future fathers of the American nation— only a deep sense of urgency.

The great problem, of course, was finances. Because it could not tax either the people or the states, Congress had no assured source of income. Its endless requests for contributions generally either met with no response or were answered by fractional payments. Yet it had had to pay for the war, which could only be done by loans from abroad. Indeed, there is some point to the assertion that the entire American effort stood or fell on the ability of Benjamin Franklin to persuade the bankers of Europe and the government of France that the war would somehow be won and the debts of the new nation paid. In 1782, foreign loans were still the only significant source of funds. But such credits balanced only a small portion of the immense debt Congress owed to American private citizens and, above all, to the army. And, of course, the foreign debt itself had to be retired. Some form of taxation was obviously an absolute necessity for national survival.

Under these circumstances Hamilton joined with the Congressional majority in an effort to secure the necessary unanimous agreement of the states to an impost on luxuries. By the summer of 1782, only Rhode Island had continued to refuse its consent. Hamilton proposed that Congress send a deputation to that state to try to secure its approval. The plan was agreed to and he was himself appointed to the committee. The effort failed, however, and Hamilton was designated by his colleagues to make a formal report to Congress and a reply to the objections of Rhode Island. The purpose of the document was not only to lay the facts before Congress but to persuade Rhode Island's legislature to change its mind. It was poorly calculated to accomplish this second purpose. Hamilton's tone was superior, at some points even arrogant. Believing that Congress ought, in fact, to be a true national government, he adopted a tone appropriate to such an institution. But since the assumption was not only false but sharply opposed by Rhode Island, the document could only be offensive to that state. That it was not taken seriously is indicated by the fact that Congress adopted it unanimously, including the vote of Rhode Island! Thereafter nothing further was heard about the matter.

But the paper was nevertheless an important one. For it stated in unambiguous terms certain of the essential constitutional doctrines Hamilton was to advocate in the future and which were to form the main principles of the Federalist party. Answering Rhode Island's objection that an impost administered, collected and dispensed by Congress would be "repugnant to the liberty of the United States," Hamilton argued that the security of the Union was the paramount concern:

> No state can dispute the obligation to pay the sum demanded without a breach of the confederation, and when the money comes into the treasury, the appropriation is the exclusive province of the Federal government. This provision of the confederation (without which it would be an empty form) comprehends in it, the principle in its fullest latitude, which the objection under consideration treats as repugnant to the liberty of the United States.

That principle was "an indefinite power of prescribing the quantity of money to be raised and of appropriating it when raised." Later Hamilton pressed the still more crucial point of implied power. "The measure in question," he wrote in the Rhode Island report, "if not within the letter is within the spirit of the confederation." On this principle was to hang the great debate over the Bank of the United States and upon it also, carried beyond the endurance of the popular majority, the Federalists were finally to make the fatal error of resting their case for the Alien and Sedition laws.

Hardly less important in the same document is Hamilton's emphasis on the sanctity of contract and the inescapable obligation of the government to pay the debts it owed to those wealthy persons who had staked the country to its capital. The capital of the debt, Hamilton noted, could only be paid off by slow degrees, but "a fund for this purpose and for paying the interest annually, on every principle of policy and justice ought to be provided. The omission will be the deepest ingratitude and cruelty to a large number of meritorious individuals, who in the most critical periods of the war have adventured their fortunes in support of our independence." It was these individuals whose interest in the future and solvency of the Union, Hamilton was later on to argue, would provide the only "cement" to save it. As a matter of principle, this plea could not be successfully answered. It served as a cornerstone in the Hamiltonian system which Jefferson and Madison were bound to respect. In the party battles of 1791–93, the Republicans were to fight against the undemocratic consequences of this principle when applied to a practical system of public finance. Their handicap was their inability to reject the principle itself. And so the American system at last came into being as Hamilton wished it.

But in 1782 there was neither a system nor the means to build one. Madison and Morris agreed warmly with Hamilton that the nation's obligations must be met and the states must somehow provide the means. While the greater part of their official effort went into preparing financial reports and records meant to impress the states, the talk in coffeehouses and cloakrooms was a mixture of cursing the states and searching for ways to break them down. Hamilton and Madison already believed that only a new constitution, or at least a radical revision of the Articles of Confederation providing undisputed power to tax, could begin to solve the national problems. But since the state of public opinion, in a natural reflex from the autocracy of England over which the war had been fought, would not permit so drastic a move, some new and more effective use must be made of the instruments at hand. Hamilton thought he saw possibilities in the still undisbanded—and unpaid—Army of the United States.

The army, as of the winter of 1782–83, had had almost no pay for three years. The states had paid the militia at least in part, and some small allotments had been made for the Continental line, but most soldiers most of the time had had no cash at all. It was no wonder that there had been stirrings of mutiny and many desertions. With the end of hostilities, though the peace treaty had not yet been signed, the mood of the soldiers was bitter beyond description. Congress was divided on whether to use hoped-for but still nonexistent funds wholly to relieve the soldiers or to pay some interest on the debt in the hope that more loans could be floated.

Hamilton saw in this situation the potentials for an effective ploy. Why not enlist the aid of the army in persuading the states to agree to a tax program? The idea, as he proposed it to Morris and Madison, was to get the anger of the army channeled behind a plan for a general national revenue—poll tax, land tax, house tax and imposts—which would put Congress in a position of solvency and enable it to pay off its obligations systematically. There is reason to believe that some members of Congress (Gouverneur Morris was one) were not averse to some overt action by the army which would frighten the states into compliance. But Hamilton had no desire to stir up strife. The better course, as he saw it, was to bring the weight of the army command into the balance in favor of the proposed taxes, implying thereby that the army saw its best hope for justice in the establishment of the national credit.

Command meant, of course, Washington. And Hamilton proceeded to broach his scheme in a private letter to the General. "The claims of the army," he wrote, "urged with moderation, but with firmness, may operate on those weak minds which are influenced by their apprehensions more than their judgments . . . they may add weight to the applications of Congress to the several states." This was a delicate matter, as Hamilton fully appreciated. The difficulty, he said, will be "to keep a *complaining* and *suffering* army" within the bounds of moderation. This was where the prestige and popularity of Washington could be brought to bear. Hamilton sought to stir Washington into action by reporting (perhaps inventing) a rumor: "An idea is propagated in the army that delicacy carried to an extreme prevents your espousing its interests with sufficient warmth. The falsehood of this opinion no one can be better acquainted with than myself; but it is not the less mischievous for being false." Hamilton, evidently, had read his Machiavelli. And he knew his prince. Only after this edgy flattery did he mention what was, in his own mind but not for Washington's understanding, the main point of the scheme. "The great *desideratum* at present is the establishment of general funds, which alone can do justice to the creditors of the United States (of whom the army forms the most meritorious class), restore public credit and supply the future wants of government."

In his reply Washington ignored both the suggestion that he was not vigorous enough in pressing the army's claims and the proposal that the army help to persuade the states to supply moneys for general purposes. He did, however, endorse Hamilton's expressions of concern for the public credit and agreed vehemently that the powers of Congress were wholly inadequate and ought to be enlarged forthwith. In the course of a month of exchanges with Hamilton, the General at one point suggested that Congress adjourn temporarily to go home and explain to their constituents the need for a stronger national government with power to raise and spend money for public purposes.

But as Washington heard more and more from other sources that Hamilton's plan was directed not so much to paying the troops as to establishing national credit by paying civilians and foreign governments, he began to suspect that he was being used, as indeed he was. Almost copying Hamilton's trick of purveying a useful rumor, Washington wrote that he would "in strict confidence, mention a matter which may be useful for you to be informed of. It is that some men (and leading ones too) in this Army, are beginning to entertain suspicions that Congress, or some members of it, regardless of the past sufferings and present distress, maugre the justice which is due them, and the returns which a grateful people should make to men who certainly have contributed more than any other class to the establishment of Independency, are to be made use of as mere Puppets to establish Continental funds; and that rather than not succeed in this measure or weaken their ground, they would make a sacrifice of the Army and all its interests."

Hamilton understood Washington's message well enough. "I thank your Excellency for the hints you are so obliging as to give me in your private letter," he wrote in reply. "I do not wonder at the suspicions that have been infused, nor should I be surprised to hear that I have been pointed out as one of the persons concerned in playing the game described." The truth was, he went on, that he did indeed favor "Continental politics." He was certain that there could be no nation without an assured public revenue and due regard for the sanctity of contract. "The necessity and discontents of the army presented themselves as a powerful engine." In fact, he told Washington, he believed so deeply in general revenue and general power to dispense it that he had voted, with the states' righters, against an impost which would have been earmarked for the payment of soldiers. His reason, however, the belief that the nation would collapse if only the soldiers were paid, was the opposite of that suggested in the rumor Washington had relayed. His commitment to the army was as strong as ever, but he would not "play off the army against the funding system." And so the matter ended.

True to his word, Hamilton presently offered a resolution, adopted by Congress, which provided the soldiers one month's pay in cash, three months' pay in certificates, and an indefinite furlough. He and Washington, as well as the other members of Congress, assumed that the soldiers would not be called back to duty. Still grumbling, but preferring something at long last to nothing, those under Washington's immediate supervision at Newburgh accepted the arrangement, were paid and went home. But those stationed in and around Philadelphia were so infuriated that they mutinied, in effect captured the capitol, and almost literally drove the Congress out of town. In the ignominy of this frantic exodus of the highest representatives of a presumably sovereign nation from their appointed place of business, Alexander Hamilton saw not only the failure of patriotism but also the weakness of republican democracy. Never afterward, though he worked as hard to shore it up as any man, did he say a kind word for popular government without effective and permanent checks upon its whims.

II

When Congress was not in session, Hamilton practiced law with as much energy as he prosecuted the public business and, for a time, with even greater distinction. Much of the year 1784 he devoted to private business. During this period he was a founder of the Bank of New York and as counsel wrote its charter. But it was as a civil liberties lawyer that he made his finest showing.

Before the Revolution, the patriot John Adams, a founder of American conservatism, had brilliantly and successfully defended British officers who had acted against the interests of the colonists. Now, after the Revolution, the patriot Alexander Hamilton, another founder of American conservatism, brilliantly and successfully defended loyalists who had acted against the interests of patriots during the war.

The problem of the loyalists was as acute in New York as had been that of the British soldiers in Boston in earlier years. New York had been occupied by the British throughout the war and loyalists had, of course, been subject to British rule. There were hundreds of cases in which loyalists had taken over and used property belonging to patriots who had fled the city. They had done so in accord with the law of the occupying power. But when the war was over and the British occupation forces gone, the situation was quickly reversed. Governor George Clinton and the Clintonian legislature enacted statutes not only to restore these properties to their original owners but to punish the loyalists with severe financial penalties—assessment for any damages that might have occurred during their occupancy and rent for the duration. From the point of view of the Revolutionary patriots it seemed little enough. But to Alexander Hamilton it seemed not only unjust in itself but to involve reliance on dangerous principles.

Under the name "Phocion," Hamilton wrote a series of pamphlets defending the loyalist cause, attacking the New York law and arguing that after a war had been settled by both arms and a treaty of peace, there should be no further discrimination as between former belligerents. Still more important, the New York law ran counter to the express terms of the peace treaty and thereby set itself above the law of the nation and the law of nations. Partly because of a concern for individual rights and partly because of his concern for national as against state sovereignty, Hamilton now broke with Clinton, with whom he had collaborated effectively during the war, and agreed to appear as defense counsel in a test case.

The case Hamilton chose to defend looked on the face of it to be hopeless. An Englishman named Waddington had occupied and operated a brewery belonging to a patriot named Rutgers from 1778 to 1783. Rutgers had been killed in the war and his widow was suing under the New York law to recover rents and damages. It was hard to imagine the court ruling against a war widow in any case, but when the statute was directed to just such cases there seemed to be no way of making a successful defense. Nevertheless, the "Phocion" letters showed how a case could be made, and *Rutgers* v. *Waddington* commanded the attention not only of the public but of the politicians and the legal profession. Mrs. Rutgers' case was argued by Egbert Benson, the state attorney general, and by Hamilton's old friend Colonel Troup, while Hamilton was assisted by Brockholst Livingston and Morgan Lewis—all of them among the foremost lawyers of the day.

Few cases in American law courts have been more learnedly or effectively argued. Hamilton rested his defense on the "law of nations," citing Vattel, Pufendorf, Grotius, etc., on the rights of belligerents in wartime and the validity of treaties regardless of the causes of war. The Rutgers' counsel argued that the American Revolution was not a war between two states but a just uprising against tyranny, and that the expropriation of which Waddington was guilty was a fair example of the kind of theft and pillage which the tyrants had carried on. The New York law was a fundamental provision to secure justice for the victims of tyranny. Since Waddington had certainly done what was charged, he was liable for the penalties. Hamilton countered by citing all the great authorities to the effect that the justice of a cause does not affect the legal status of belligerents.

Further, and more significantly, Hamilton stressed the fact that the national government, the Continental Congress, acting under its undoubted authority as granted in the Articles of Confederation to conduct the foreign policy of the country, had entered into a solemn treaty with the British, meeting them at Paris as co-belligerents. Under the treaty there were to be no reprisals against British or American citizens. Thus the New York law could have no sanction since it was in evident violation of the treaty of peace.

Finally, Hamilton advanced the notion that the court had the power and duty to determine whether the statute was in accord with the federal constitution. If not, then it was void, since the Articles of Confederation and treaties made under them were the supreme law of the land.

The court, consisting of the mayor and aldermen of the City of New York, compromised the case as was politically expedient. But they allowed most of Hamilton's plea. They ordered Waddington to pay rents for the years 1778–80, before martial law had been established, but decided he need not pay for 1780–83. They held that the Congress did indeed have sovereign authority over foreign relations and that treaties were the "supreme law of the land." Further, they agreed that no state could alter or abridge the Articles or act in any way contrary to the treaty of peace. They did not accept Hamilton's statement of the doctrine of judicial review, however, holding, sententiously, that legislatures decide what the law is to be and whether it is valid, not courts. Since this passage was in flat contradiction to the decision they were taking, it is apparent that they thought it politically expedient to disavow any superiority to the state legislature. Hamilton was well satisfied.

III

But victories in law courts were no substitute for a viable national government. If the Articles were the supreme law where they granted powers to Congress, the trouble was that, except for foreign affairs, they granted Congress almost no effective powers at all. And so the problem of building the nation remained.

The condition of the country was nearly chaotic. Bankruptcy and inflation characterized the economic situation, while political pots boiled everywhere, and sorely pressed farmers, especially in New England, were in a mood for rebellion. Under these circumstances Hamilton, Madison, Gouverneur Morris and others succeeded in getting Congress to call for a special convention to clarify and strengthen the powers of Congress over trade and commerce.

Hamilton hoped and worked for quick action. He frankly feared the temper of the people. His passion for order was daily being countered by what he called "the rage for liberty." He had always feared the undisciplined feelings and ambitions loosed by the Revolution. In peacetime they were doubly dangerous. He was no social revolutionist, and he never sought to conceal the fact. The war with Britain, in his view, had been a struggle for independence warranted because Great Britain insisted upon exercising "unconstitutional" authority. It was not intended to bring about any profound changes in the social structure of America.

The contrast between Hamilton's essential conservatism and Jefferson's essential liberalism is nowhere more evident than in the interpretation of the Revolution. To Jefferson the prime objective of the war was the rights of man. No sooner had independence been proclaimed than he returned to Virginia to take the lead in revising the laws of that state in order to emancipate individual citizens from the vestiges of feudalism— primogeniture and entail—and to guarantee equal rights and popular participation in government. Contrast Hamilton's concern:

> The circumstances of a revolution quickened the public sensibility on every point connected with the security of popular rights, and in some instances raised the warmth of our zeal beyond the degree which consisted with the due temperature of the body politic.

He wished, he said, to secure "a happy mean" between too much liberty and too much government—a desire that would no doubt have been shared by Jefferson as it certainly was by Madison. But the two Virginians would always be prepared to sacrifice order for liberty if necessary, while Hamilton would sacrifice not all, but a good deal of liberty to obtain order and strength in the state.*

---

* In recent years, scholars like Louis Hartz (*The Liberal Tradition in America,* 1955), Clinton Rossiter (*Seedtime of the Republic,* 1953) and Daniel Boorstin (*The Genius of American Politics,* 1955) have restated Hamilton's attitude as though it were a description of the Revolution itself in their effort to show that the war for independence was essentially a conservative action. For the view that the war was at the same time a profound social and political revolution, see Franklin Jameson, *The American Revolution* (1922), Arthur Schlesinger, Jr., *The Vital Center*

Conflicting attitudes toward the Society of the Cincinnati is an interesting case in point. This society of Revolutionary War officers was intended by its founders to sustain the patriotism that had won the war and hoped to hold the nation together. Washington was the founding president. It was an exclusive body which was to be perpetuated by the inheritance of membership, the succession going from eldest son to eldest son. Jefferson attacked it as soon as he learned of it, denouncing it as suggesting distinctions of nobility and appropriate not to a republic but to an aristocracy. Jefferson's view was widely shared and there was a great deal of criticism of the Society both on the floors of state legislatures and in the press. Jefferson even took up the matter with Washington personally, urging him to have the aristocratic elements of the charter removed. Washington was sufficiently alarmed by the popular reaction to urge that primogeniture in the Society be abolished, and suggested other reforms. Hamilton, active in the New York chapter, stood firm for the Society. He agreed that primogeniture was a mistaken means of perpetuating the organization, but he insisted that it should nevertheless be perpetuated. He did not shy at the charge of forming a noble order. So long as all members became so on "merit," he argued, the aims of the Society were so vital to the nation that it should be perpetuated. In the Cincinnati, Jefferson saw the danger of subversion to the republic; Hamilton saw in the same body a likely pillar of stability and order.

At any rate, it was certainly to secure strength and order that Hamilton and the other delegates met at Annapolis in September, 1786, to revise the commercial powers of the United States under the Articles of Confederation. The commissioners were assembled for a strictly limited purpose. But as Hamilton saw the matter, any concerted action in the name of the nation which the states would approve was a step toward building the nation. To secure the powers of Congress

(1949), Dumas Malone, *Jefferson and the Rights of Man* (1951) and Stuart Gerry Brown, *The First Republicans* (1954) and "Democracy, the New Conservatism, and the Liberal Tradition in America," *Ethics*, LXVI, 1 (October, 1955).

over both domestic commerce and international trade would
be helpful in itself and could have significant implications for
expanding the powers of the central government.

It was doubly frustrating to Hamilton, therefore, that a
quorum could not be assembled even for the limited purposes
approved by Congress and the state legislatures. With only five
states present, the Annapolis convention was powerless to act.
But Hamilton and others were unwilling simply to give up and
go home. Strongly supported by Tench Coxe of Pennsylvania,
by Edmund Randolph and James Monroe of Virginia, and by
the whole delegation of New Jersey, Hamilton drafted a report
on the abortive session, unanimously adopted by the commissioners, which was in effect a call for a constitutional convention.

Hamilton's draft is said to have been modified as to tone
and bluntness at the insistence of Randolph, then Governor of
Virginia. However, the document remained direct enough.
After a suitable apology for exceeding their instructions, the
commissioners expressed the opinion that "the idea of extend-
ing the powers of their deputies, to other objects," as the State
of New Jersey had already authorized, was "an improvement
on the original plan." The commissioners did not elaborate on
the "defects" of the Articles of Confederation, but called
instead for "a deliberate and candid discussion . . . which will
unite the sentiments of all the states." The best way would be
to hold a national convention. They asked the concurrence of
the states "in the appointment of Commissioners to meet at
Philadelphia on the second Monday in May next, to take into
consideration the situation of the United States, to devise such
further provisions as shall appear to them necessary to render
the constitution of the federal government adequate to the
exigencies of the Union." This report was sent not only to the
legislatures of the states represented at Annapolis (Virginia,
Delaware, Pennsylvania, New Jersey and New York) but,
"from motives of respect, to the executives of the other states."

No one can say whether this call would have won the
consent of the legislatures, embroiled as they were in problems
they thought of as their own and jealous of any superior body
that might come into being, had not Daniel Shays of Massa-

chusetts chosen that moment to lead his rebellion against constituted authority. What is certain is that state legislators, all over the country, were frightened out of their parochial immersion into doing precisely what men like Hamilton, Madison, Washington and the two Morrises had for years been telling them had to be done. They called the convention for the second Monday in May at Philadelphia, as the Annapolis commissioners had urged, and thus took the second long stride toward building the nation—the Revolution itself having been the first.

IV

On the record of his life thus far it might well have been expected that Alexander Hamilton would play a leading role, if not *the* leading role, in the convention he had been urging and working toward since before the end of the war. But the convention of 1787 at Philadelphia was one of the supreme *political* achievements of modern history, and precisely because its quality was political, Hamilton was effectively disqualified in advance from leading it.

If one might reasonably suppose that Hamilton would have grasped the significance of Randolph's caution at Annapolis, the grudging assent of the majority Clintonians in his own state, and the calm but earnest counsel of his friend Madison to accept the limits of the possible at Philadelphia, one must nevertheless recollect the posture of intellectual superiority Hamilton had adopted as long before as his quarrel with Washington. He had been elected to the New York legislature by the anti-Clinton faction. But as a minority member he confined his efforts, after Annapolis, to arguing for the federal impost, otherwise holding himself somewhat aloof from the politics of the legislative hall. At Philadelphia, he seems to have decided, he would be "above" politics. He would tell the delegates from the thirteen states, in plain language once and for all, that any continuing to pander to the masses would seriously risk the very existence of the nation, that public order would depend on public confidence and that public confidence, in turn, could only be obtained by a government so strong and so firmly entrenched that it would not be shaken or frightened by the Daniel Shayses of the future. In short, though it was certainly not his intention, Hamilton decided to say as persuasively as he could all the things which, in the polemics of the coming years, would be charged against him to prove he was a monarchist. He was not a monarchist, in practice, then or ever. But the position he adopted was so unfriendly to popular government that he immobilized himself as an effective force in a convention dominated by men as politically skillful—and dedicated—as Madison, Franklin, Randolph and James Wilson. Hamilton's great service to the Constitution—unsurpassed by any of the Founding Fathers—was to come after it had been drafted, not during the days of deliberation.

This is not to say that Hamilton played an insignificant part at Philadelphia. His two appearances—he absented himself for a great part of the time—were bold enough to stir others to practical agreement, and in the end he fell loyally into step behind Madison.

It is not necessary to review the familiar story of the Constitutional Convention in order to give a fair account of Hamilton's life. But it is of the first importance to go carefully through his one full-dress speech to the delegates and the plan he at that time offered. There are several surviving versions of the speech, differing among themselves in a number of ways. On the essential points, however, Madison, Yates, Lansing and King agree. Hamilton's own notes are sketchy and do not actually cover all that his listeners agree that he said, but they do contain the cardinal points.

At any rate, on June 18, Hamilton set forth his views in unforgettable terms—and his political opponents never allowed him to forget! As a basic principle he laid it down that the people are the "source of government," but since they are "unreasonable," have conflicting interests as "debtors and creditors, etc.," there ought to be a principle in government capable of resisting the popular current. For such a purpose "no periodical duration" would do. If it is granted on all sides that there is to be a popularly elected assembly, the second body, meant to check the first, must not suffer from the defects of the first. If the Senate (checking the popular assembly) were to have seven-year terms, for example, one-seventh of the members would always have only one year remaining to serve and "seeing their dissolution approach, they will sacrifice." So it would be with any set term in which a portion of the members rotated, as had been proposed by other delegates. The only solution was to have senators serve "during good behavior," that is, for life. A permanent seat would enable a senator to act in the national interest on all matters, not merely "in ordinary cases, in which there is no strong public passion; but . . . in cases where there is." The British House of Lords was a case in point. It is a "most noble institution," Hamilton told the Convention. "Having nothing to hope for by a change, and a sufficient interest by means of their property, in being faithful to the national interest, they form a permanent barrier against every pernicious innovation."

Turning to the Executive, Hamilton presented a similar view. An Executive elected by the people for a stated term would be tempted to intrigue for reelection. If he was expected to check the democratic power of the assembly, he could not do it because he would himself be dependent on the popular will. The Executive—in his own notes Hamilton used the word "monarch"—ought, he said, "to be hereditary, and to have so much power, that it will not be his interest to risk much to acquire more." Another important advantage is that a monarch "is above corruption," and "must always intend, in respect to foreign nations, the true interest and glory of the people." Hamilton recited the record of some early republics to argue that republican government, in contrast to monarchy, is "liable to foreign corruption and intrigue." As he delivered the speech, according to Madison's version, Hamilton amended these notes to make his Executive elective for life, rather than hereditary, and avoided the term "monarch." In fact, he took pains to anticipate criticism that his position was monarchist:

It will be objected probably, that such an Executive will be an *elective Monarch,* and will give birth to the tumults which characterize that form of government. He would reply that *Monarch* is an indefinite term. It marks not either the degree or duration of power. If this Executive Magistrate would be a monarch for life—the other proposed by the Report from the Committee of the whole, would be a monarch for seven years.

Finally, Hamilton told the delegates frankly that he knew he was stating an unacceptable position, "beyond the ideas of most members." But if his plan could not be adopted, he wanted to know whether the Virginia plan, with Randolph as its spokesman, would fare any better. He guessed that the people would "adopt neither." But there were, he said, "evils operating in the States which must soon cure the people of their fondness for democracies. . . ." In time, he argued, "the people will be unshackled from their prejudices; and whenever that happens, they will themselves not be satisfied at stopping where the plan of Mr. Randolph would place them, but be ready to go at least as far as he [Hamilton] proposes."

Meanwhile, he had prepared a sketch of an alternative plan for the consideration of the delegates. This he read to the Convention, not as a formal motion, but, as he put it, "to suggest the amendments which he should probably propose to the plans of Mr. Randolph." The plan called for all legislative power to be vested in a two-house legislature with a lower house popularly elected and a senate elected to serve during "good behavior." The Executive, likewise, was to be elected to serve during "good behavior." Both the Executive, called "Governor," and the senators were to be chosen by electors, who, in turn, were to be chosen by the people. The Executive was to have all administrative power with an absolute veto over legislation. Judicial power was to be vested in a supreme federal court, which was also to serve during good behavior. The states were to be subordinated to the federal government by the legal system, and state governors were to be appointed by "the general government." This latter provision, taken together with some remarks Hamilton made in his address, seemed to call for the practical elimination of the state sovereignties. Hamilton, on twenty-four hours of reflection, decided he did not wish to go so far and took the floor to deny an intention of "extinguishing" the states.

None of the various accounts of the Convention suggests that Hamilton's colleagues were shocked or disturbed by his plan—or by his speech. No doubt they were already sufficiently familiar with his views from informal conversations. What they did was to ignore it. Discussion of the Randolph plan presently recommenced. Hamilton offered amendments, which were duly rejected. On June 29, he went home, ostensibly to attend to private business but perhaps also because he felt himself out of the center of power in the Convention. He did not return until some time around the thirteenth of August, when he next took part in the debates.

By that time the Virginia plan had been amended to the satisfaction of most of the delegates. The remaining work was chiefly in detail and in sharpening and polishing of language. Hamilton played a prominent part at this stage, but not so great as Gouverneur Morris or James Wilson. These men, with assistance at various points from others, gave final form to the structure of which Madison was the acknowledged chief architect. When Madison and Hamilton renewed their collaboration in the fall and winter, the roles were reversed, as Hamilton took the lead in the great campaign for adoption of the draft by the states, while Madison worked closely and effectively under his leadership.

The political consequences of Hamilton's June 18 speech were to come later—indeed, many years later. But it is important to recognize that at the Convention itself Hamilton had reason to believe that his remarks would not have political consequences at all. For one thing, the proceedings were conducted behind closed doors; there was firm agreement that everything said on the floor was privileged. There was no official record, no stenographer. No one except the delegates themselves was allowed on the floor. Another reason for Hamilton to believe that his confidence would be kept was that many delegates made no secret of their fear of democracy and their determination to keep it out of the United States. The Founding Fathers, in short, were not at that stage revolutionists. The Revolution was long over. And these delegates were, for the most part, men of property and position anxious to stabilize the nation and provide it with a chance to grow.

They were seeking ways to secure the performance of contracts, public as well as private, to put the country on a sound financial basis, and to tie the states together by their common interests. They were not thinking about individual liberties or social change except, perhaps, as claims to be minimized. Under such conditions Hamilton was not nearly so extreme as he was to seem in after years. If few of the delegates were as antagonistic to democracy as Hamilton was, and none at least openly friendly to monarchy, none, at the moment, thought him subversive. Jefferson, far away in Paris, would certainly have been shocked and angered, but he was not informed and, in any case, his liberal revolutionary ideas were not at that juncture in the main current of American thought. Neither were Hamilton's archconservative views. But the New Yorker was a good deal closer to it than was his future rival.

v

On September 17, the Constitution was signed and published. Hamilton was a signer. The cautious Randolph, interestingly enough, was not. The Virginia governor went home and sampled public opinion for weeks before finally deciding to side with the federal forces at the Virginia ratifying convention. The only other delegates who refused to sign were the veteran patriots Elbridge Gerry of Massachusetts and George Mason of Virginia, both unwilling to support a document without a bill of personal rights.

Back in New York and Albany, Hamilton found the press full of vigorous attacks on the new plan of government. The Clinton faction gave every indication that they would oppose its ratification, and anti-federalists contested elections to the ratifying convention with considerable bitterness. The undemocratic—better, perhaps, nondemocratic—elements of the draft plan were the object of the attack, while no one seemed prepared to speak up enthusiastically for its adoption. Hamilton, under these circumstances, sought means to produce a more favorable climate of opinion. According to an oft-repeated if not well-authenticated story, he was on the boat from Albany to New York when the idea for *The Federalist* came to him.

He is said to have gone to his cabin and dashed off the first number of his masterpiece in time to give it to the *Independent Journal* as soon as the boat docked.

Over the signature "Publius," Hamilton addressed the people of New York, hoping through them to reach the delegates to the forthcoming convention:

> After an unequivocal experience of the inefficacy of the subsisting Federal Government, you are called upon to deliberate on a new Constitution for the United States of America. The subject speaks its own importance; comprehending in its consequences, nothing less than the existence of the UNION, the safety and welfare of the parts of which it is composed, the fate of an empire, in many respects the most interesting in the world. It has been frequently remarked, that it seems to have been reserved to the people of this country, by their conduct and example, to decide the important question, whether societies of men are really capable or not, of establishing good government from reflection and choice, or whether they are forever to depend, for their political constitutions, on accident and force. If there be any truth in the remark, the crisis at which we are arrived, may with propriety be regarded as the era in which that decision is to be made; and a wrong election of the part we shall act, may, in this view, deserve to be considered the general misfortune of mankind.

So, in effect, began the most brilliant constitutional debate in history, and the one great American book of political theory. That it should have been commenced and in large part written by a man who doubted the very basis of the cause he was defending—who did not trust the people to whom he was appealing—is more than an irony of history, it is a measure of the remarkable patriotism and driving character of Alexander Hamilton. What was paramount to him was the nation. If it was not to be governed as he wished it to be and deeply believed it ought to be if it was to succeed, at least it must be governed *as a nation.* The proposed Constitution would make that possible. The draft plan was rather more than the lesser of two evils. It represented the difference between having some chance to build a nation and having none. Hamilton, at the height of his intellectual powers, now gave all his heart and all his energy to securing that chance.

The first number of *The Federalist* appeared on October 27, 1787, the last on May 28, 1788. There were eighty-five numbers in all, published at the rate of two or three a week and gathered in the closing stages into two bound volumes for general distribution throughout the country. At the outset Hamilton enlisted the help of Madison, John Jay and William Duer. Duer's two pieces have never been included in the published volumes, and Jay, who became ill in November, wrote only Nos. 2–5, and 64. The authorship of some fifteen of the papers has never been positively determined, though most of them are probably by Hamilton. What is certain is that Madison wrote Nos. 10, 14 and 37–58, while Hamilton contributed Nos. 1, 6–9, 11–13, 15–17, 21–36, 59–61 and 65–85, much the largest share. If Nos. 10 and 39, on factions (parties) and the definition of republican government, established Madison's reputation as the great American philosopher of the democratic process, Hamilton's contributions revealed him as the master builder.

As these papers appeared, often in as many as four newspapers at once, they were more and more widely discussed. Through them not only the public in general but the delegates to the New York convention got an education in the nature of government. The legislature, it should be noted, had authorized all males of twenty-one and over, regardless of property holdings, to vote in the election of delegates held in January. "Publius" thus addressed a democratic electorate, one of the first in America, indeed, in the modern world.

The intricacies of legislation, the techniques of administration, the balancing force of the judiciary were analyzed in detail as each article of the Constitution was subjected to careful and, of course, favorable consideration. Above all, the efficacy of a government combining the expression of the popular will with the steady hand of sanctioned authority was progressively displayed in these papers and shown to be preferable, from the vantage points of both freedom and order, to any other system. Classic authorities were from time to time cited, and the whole work no doubt owes something to the Aristotelian tradition of constitutionalism, but the emphasis was on the practical, on the kinds of questions citizens were asking and the kinds of objections to be expected at the ratifying convention.

The New York convention organized with a quorum at Poughkeepsie on June 18, 1788, and debated until July 26, when it ratified the Constitution by a vote of 30–27. When the convention assembled, eight states had already ratified, so that New York could have provided the decisive ninth vote. But before New York acted, two other states, including Virginia, had ratified, so that the Constitution was adopted without the vote of New York.

The long delay of the New York convention was partly owing to the strategy of delegate Alexander Hamilton. When the convention sat down there was, as Hamilton knew there would be, a substantial anti-federal majority, reflecting the view of Governor Clinton. If a vote had been taken in the early stages, New York would certainly have rejected the Constitution, perhaps giving encouragement to anti-federalists elsewhere. On the other hand, if action could be postponed by prolonging the debate, not only might some delegates waver but Virginia, led by Washington and Madison, might ratify and thereby powerfully influence New York. The strategy worked well. The debate itself, in which Hamilton played a major part, split the Clinton faction, and Virginia's ratification, on June 25, came as decisive news. New York could and did clamor for amendments, even for a new convention, but she was not going to be left out.

As for Hamilton, nothing he said in the debates at Poughkeepsie added substantially to what he had already written in *The Federalist* essays. But his patience was exemplary, if unaccustomed, and in the taverns after the day's deliberations he took pains to ingratiate himself with any Clintonians who appeared to be uncertain—and there were several. It was a political performance of a high order by an essentially non-political person. He was never again either to display so amenable a disposition or to marshal his political troops with such skill. His motives, of course, were by this time transparent. He wanted to get rid of the flabby arrangement that had for so long struggled impossibly to be a national government. He wanted to put in its place an unquestioned sovereign. The Constitution was the means at hand. Yet in the next years, when it was a matter of building on the blueprint and when his motives to personal success were certainly stronger, his temper simply would not let him exercise for political purposes the charm he always had at his command. Had he shown as Secretary of the Treasury the patience and deference to colleagues and members of Congress he showed in the New York convention, the political history of his era and of his country's future might well have been different—if not as exciting.

The New York convention marked the height of Hamilton's popularity, though not his power. In New York City the federalists celebrated his triumph with a parade down Broadway led by a float of the "Good Ship Alexander Hamilton." On the prow was the Colonel's figure holding the Constitution in his hand. The symbol was fair enough, though some Clintonians sneered as it passed by.

Chapter 3

SECRETARY OF THE TREASURY: THE HAMILTONIAN SYSTEM

I

The Constitution once adopted, the next pressing question was the quality of the men who were to hold office. Hamilton, not only working with such Eastern federalists as John Jay and Rufus King but keeping up his alliance with Madison, led the effort to persuade Washington to accept the Presidency. "I am not sure," he wrote the General, "that your refusal would not throw everything into confusion." He told Washington that there would be a "general call of your country," and took it for granted Washington would "comply." Washington, for his part, once more treating Hamilton as his political intimate, confessed his devout wish for retirement. However, if it "were ever indispensable a different line should be adopted," Washington trusted Hamilton and "some others" to understand that it was patriotism and not inconsistency which would alter his judgment.

As evidence mounted that the anti-federalists were still strong and still unfriendly to the Constitution, Hamilton appealed to Washington, in effect, to save the situation. "Your signature to the proposed system," he said, "pledges your judgment for its being such an one as upon the whole was worthy of the public approbation." Now there was the prospect that "it should miscarry." Washington alone could make sure that it would succeed. "This view of the subject," Hamilton urged, "will suggest to your mind greater hazard to that fame, which must be and ought to be dear to you, in refusing your future aid to the system than in affording it. I will only add that in my estimate of the matter that aid is indispensable."

At the time of this correspondence Madison was in New York, meeting regularly with Hamilton on the floor of Congress and in private sharing the effort to secure Washington's election. When Madison returned to Virginia, Hamilton kept him informed of developments in the North and East and counted on his support for the election of federalist members of the House and Senate and of John Adams as Vice-President. It was Madison who warned him that there was a move under way to name George Clinton Vice-President instead of Adams. But Hamilton did not take this too seriously. A canvass of the states indicated that there would not be enough anti-federalist votes in the Electoral College to enable anyone to beat Adams. In any case, he told Madison, he did not think that Clinton "would be disposed to exchange his present appointment for that office or to risk his popularity by holding both." In the same letter he advised Madison to run for the House of Representatives, though he would have preferred to see his friend "in one of the Executive departments." The trouble was that it appeared that the membership of the House would be "defective in characters of a certain description." That is, there would not be enough trustworthy federalists. Madison would be needed to hold firm for the Constitution and the Union in the lower house. "Might I advise it would be that you bent your course to Virginia." Madison did so, presently becoming the leader of the First Congress, where his unanticipated but inevitable break with Hamilton was soon to take place.

Meanwhile, in New York politics Hamilton took an active part in the effort to defeat Clinton for reelection as governor. As a member of the committee to elect Robert Yates governor and Philip Van Cortlandt lieutenant governor, he addressed several printed communications to the voters at large. The burden of these messages was the anti-federalism of Clinton rather than the merits of the candidates Hamilton was supporting.

But of greater importance was a series of twelve letters

signed "H. G." which appeared in the *Daily Advertiser,* addressed to a fictitious farmer in Suffolk County. These letters marked Hamilton's return to the endless pamphlet wars. In them he reviewed Clinton's record from the beginning of the Revolution. His tactic was to accord the Governor a measure of praise in each letter and then to counterbalance the praise with devastating reports of his failures and shortcomings. Clinton had been, for example, a patriot general in the war, but he had commanded the Union forces during the burning and sacking of Esopus (later Kingston, New York) by the British in 1777. He had been an energetic and patriotic governor thereafter, but his inefficiency and striving for personal popularity had cost the rebel cause dearly. He had been against the British with all his heart, but when the war was over he became an enemy of the Union . . . etc., etc. By such writing Hamilton invited, and received, abundance of polemical denunciation by Clinton's followers, much of it scurrilous. From this futile effort against Clinton, who was easily re-elected, Hamilton was almost continuously engaged for the rest of his life in controversies of this kind. Often he could justifiably relish the sharp and polished phrase with which he damned his political enemies, but seldom or never could he boast of victories that might fairly be said to have been worth the fund of energy he expended on them.

II

With Washington and Adams duly elected, the Congress under the new Constitution set to work to establish by law the judiciary and executive departments of the government. Since they were sitting in New York, Hamilton was in close daily contact with Madison and other members, including his father-in-law, who was a senator from New York. To what extent his ideas for the Treasury were written into the law establishing that department is not known, but there is every reason to believe that both the Congress and the President consulted Hamilton in the course of their deliberations.

What is certain is that Washington consulted Hamilton on the delicate subject of the conduct of his own office. After nearly two hundred years of the American Presidency, now so familiar everywhere, it is difficult to go back in imagination to the spring of 1789, when no such office had ever before existed anywhere. The President was to have very great powers, but these were to be checked by the other branches of the government. He was to be the chief of state, but he was not a king as were all the chiefs of state of the old world. What should be the etiquette governing his own conduct and the conduct of those around him, as well as the public? Jefferson, still in France, was not consulted. Had his views been sought, he would no doubt have counseled simplicity and democracy, doing away with all vestiges of old-world ceremonial. But men like Adams and Alexander Hamilton, on the scene and in a position to influence Washington's decisions, were not democrats. In their view the Presidency was to be the central symbol of the new nation's dignity before the world, and of the deference which ought to be paid to it by the people of the United States. For such purposes they considered ceremony of great importance. Adams, going beyond the bounds of common sense, proposed to address the President as "Your Highness." Ironically, Hamilton, who was more of a monarchist than Adams, made the suggestions which were adopted.

The President, Hamilton told Washington, ought to be addressed as "Your Excellency," a form signifying the highest respect, yet not smacking of European courts. On the other hand, Hamilton used the royalist term "levee" for the weekly receptions he advised the President to hold—"an hour to be fixed at which it shall be understood that [the President] will appear and consequently that the visitors are previously to be assembled." "The President," he suggested, should "remain half an hour, in which time he may converse cursorily on indifferent subjects with such persons as shall strike his attention." Hamilton's foresight told him rightly that "some regulation will be hereafter necessary to designate those who may visit." The problem of regulating the flow of the President's visitors has become more rather than less serious with the years. Men like Jefferson and Polk, even Lincoln to a degree, tended to receive anyone who came to the door, but more

commonly Presidents have depended on someone, regardless
of his title, to act as an appointments secretary. Hamilton
added to his recommendation for "levees" that "no visits were
to be returned." His advice was taken. In early years Presidents did not return calls for form's sake; later it became in
any case a physical impossibility.

In his suggestion that Washington limit himself to at most
four formal entertainments a year "on the anniversaries of
important events in the Revolution," he revealed that his
models were indeed the European courts. The guest list, he
said, ought to be strictly limited to foreign ministers and department heads, judges and members of the Senate of the
United States. He likened the latter body to the House of
Lords and proposed frankly to elevate senators above members of the House. Even at the private dinners, Hamilton
would restrict the guest list to "members of the legislature
and other official characters." The President, in short, was to
have no personal social life. While most Presidents have refused to accept such narrow constraints on their activities, it
is nevertheless an important burden of the office that they
cannot maintain close personal relations with persons outside
the government—or in it!—without risking political jealousies
which may overbalance the satisfactions of friendship. Men
like Grant and Truman were seriously hurt politically by the
cupidity and ineptitude of personal friends, and even so sophisticated a President as John Kennedy could be embarrassed
when published stories by his personal friends among the
Washington press corps were directed against such important
associates as U.N. Ambassador Adlai E. Stevenson. Hamilton's
foresight at least saved Washington from annoyances of this
sort.

To the contrary, following Hamilton's advice, Washington
ran no such risks. Not only did he maintain the full distance
from others that was expected of a chief of state, but he
adopted many of the manners characteristic of the courts of
Europe, even to the carriage with coat of arms and liveried
footmen. And almost immediately his house and entourage
were designated as a "court" by the press. Those who were
privileged to take a place in it tended to welcome the idea,

while anti-federalists on the outside quickly began to whisper and cavil against the revival of monarchy. Not without reason. When Mrs. Washington arrived at New York, the *Gazette of the United States* reported the event as though she were a queen. "The Lady of his Excellency the Governor, Lady Sterling, Lady Mary Watts, Lady Kitty Duer, La Marchioness de Brehan, the ladies of the Most Honorable Mr. Langdon, and the Most Honorable Mr. Dalton" were, said the paper, among those who "paid their devoirs to the amiable consort of our beloved President."

While Alexander and Betsy Hamilton were at the center of this society and among its most fashionable hosts at their Wall Street home, Alexander was far more concerned with what went on beneath the trappings of state. The trappings he favored for very practical political reasons. Set Washington on a pedestal where he would be an object of national reverence and there would have to be a nation to pay him deference. With the adulation and the genuine respect would go the power, not specified or intended by the Constitution, to determine the national policy, persuade the Congress to pass the bills and the people to accept them. If the nation was to grow to full authority over the states and the people, Washington would be the means. Let him, therefore, live and act like a king. If Hamilton never said so in so many words, there is no doubt that he thought of himself as prime minister.

And so, in effect, he presently became. On September 11, 1789, the President, on the advice of Madison and Robert Morris, sent Hamilton's name to the Senate to be Secretary of the Treasury. His appointment was confirmed unanimously the same day. It was certainly no accident that Hamilton was the first to be nominated by Washington for a Cabinet post. For the next five years he superintended the reconstruction of the nation's credit, built up a system of public administration, involved himself deeply in foreign policy matters, directed the federalist faction in Congress, founded a political party and served generally as principal adviser to the President. It is probably safe to say that no other Cabinet officer in American history ever so nearly approximated the role of prime minister.

In *Federalist* No. 72 Hamilton had written:

> The persons . . . to whose immediate management these
> different [administrative] matters are committed, ought
> to be considered as the assistants or deputies of the chief
> magistrate, and on this account, they ought to derive
> their offices from his appointment, at least from his nom-
> ination, and ought to be subject to his superintendence.

Under this principle Hamilton entered his new office. Especially in the early months he took up directly with the President
many matters of detail. Congress passed very specific laws
directing or authorizing the President to do this or that,
which, in turn, he delegated to the Secretary of the Treasury.
Except for such routine matters as keeping the public books
and issuing circular orders to treasury agents—tax collectors,
customs officials, etc.—Hamilton kept the President informed
on all substantive matters proceeding in his department.

But Hamilton was able to leave a great deal to his staff, the
largest and most talented in the new government, small though
it seems by the standards of the twentieth century. In the
time thus freed, the Secretary bent his efforts to devising plans
and policy. The immediate incentive was a resolution of the
House of Representatives (September 21, 1789), stimulated
by himself, calling on the Secretary of the Treasury to prepare
a plan for "an adequate provision for the support of the
public credit." This was not a matter of careful administrative subordination to the President; it was the opportunity he
had waited for for many years to devise and advocate, with
the authority of high office, a national economic policy.

On January 9, 1790, Alexander Hamilton addressed his report to the House of Representatives:

> The Secretary of the Treasury, in obedience to the res-
> olution of the House of Representatives, of the twenty-
> first day of September last, has, during the recess of Con-

gress, applied himself to the consideration of a proper
plan for the support of the public credit, with all the
attention which was due to the authority of the House,
and to the magnitude of the object.

What followed showed how well adapted to the "magnitude" of
the subject were the magnitude of Hamilton's knowledge and
the scope of his imagination. This *First Report on the Public
Credit,* as it came to be known, remains one of the best-drawn
state papers ever offered by an American statesman, as well
as the landmark document which opened to the surface those
divisions of opinion which were to galvanize factions into the
American party system.

The basis of Hamilton's proposal was the funding of the
war debts. As he saw it, the government had really only two
alternatives: repudiate the debt, or pay it at face value. Re-
pudiation was unthinkable, since the public credit would
thereby be destroyed, not supported. To continue in the present chaotic state was equally unthinkable. There remained
only the alternative of systematic funding. This meant that the
government would recall all the paper issued by the Confederation Congress and redeem it in bonds of varying dates
of maturity and bearing fair interest rates. In computing the
ratio of new bonds (Hamilton referred to them as "stock")
to old paper, accumulated interest would be included.

Such a funded debt, Hamilton argued, would be a public
benefit. It would obviously be advantageous to holders of old
government paper and to restoring American credit abroad; it
would also be helpful to farmers, traders and manufacturers,
since it would not only stabilize the money market but provide a useful medium of exchange, "a substitute for money."
Anyone who cashes a Series E U.S. Treasury bond today is
illustrating Hamilton's point. The values of land, he suggested,
had fallen by as much as 50 percent in some areas, largely
because of the shortage of cash. In a market starved for
money, the owner who wished to sell land had to take what
he could get. The same principle held to a degree in the fields
of commerce and manufacture. A fresh supply of money
would stimulate the entire economic system. A recovered

economy would yield a much greater harvest of tax revenues, so that the costs of the debt would diminish. As securities were found to be worth the interest promised, and as they were systematically redeemed on the dates established, the credit of the United States would be forever secured.

If the national debt was to be funded, there arose the vexing question whether there should be a discrimination between present and original holders of Confederation securities. There had been a good deal of popular and newspaper discussion of this point from the moment of the adoption of the Constitution, when it began to seem possible that these securities would be redeemed. Many people who had originally bought Confederation paper, during the war especially, had been forced to sell for what they could get as the market value declined to almost nothing—"not worth a Continental." Others, of course, had bought the notes cheap on pure speculation. With the funding of the debt, the latter would reap an immense profit, while the former would get nothing, though it was they who had put their property at the disposal of the Revolution. Hamilton recognized their claim as ideally worthy. But it seemed to him simply not feasible in practice. He cited two principles against discrimination. The old Congress, he reminded the new, had resolved

> "that to discriminate the merits of these several descriptions of creditors, would be a task equally unnecessary and invidious. If the voice of humanity plead more loudly in favor of some than of others, the voice of policy, no less than of justice, pleads in favor of all. A Wise Nation will never permit those who relieve the wants of their country, or who *rely most* on its *faith,* its *firmness,* and its *resources,* when either of them is distrusted to suffer by the event."

The italics Hamilton added for his purpose. For his second principle he appealed to the Constitution:

> . . . all debts contracted and engagements entered into before the adoption of that Constitution shall be as valid

against the United States under it, as under the Confederation.

Hamilton had himself had a part in writing both these documents, and so had Madison. When the great debate on discrimination presently erupted, the latter no doubt looked at
such passages ruefully. But Hamilton himself was to be
trapped some years later when Jefferson quoted the second
passage against his effort to discriminate between the governments of France under the monarchy and under the republic.

After disposing of the discrimination question, Hamilton
went on to make a still more controversial proposal: that the
state debts should be assumed by the national government,
thus channeling the flow of tax revenues to the discharge of a
single nationally funded debt. This plan was certain to divide
the states. Some few had already paid off all or most of their
debts; some had paid a large portion; others had paid almost
nothing at all. To the first class, assumption looked more like
confiscation. How could one justify taxing people of one state
to pay the debts of another? States in the third class could
answer the question easily: since all had contracted debts for
the common defense, it was reasonable for all to share in
their redemption. Those who had neither fully paid nor failed
to make provision were caught in the proverbial middle, un-
sure whether it would be more or less costly to them to have
the state debts assumed by the national government.

Hamilton's reasons for proposing assumption were three-
fold: (1) to avoid competition between the federal government and the states for tax revenue; (2) to promote systematic
rather than uneven development of agriculture and industry;
(3) to bind the creditors to the national government. Of these
the last was certainly first in Hamilton's mind. It was a central element in building the nation. "If all the public creditors," he wrote, "receive their dues from one source, distributed with an equal hand, their interest will be the same.
And having the same interests, they will unite in the support
of the fiscal arrangements of the government." Here, in fact,
is the essence of the Hamiltonian system, and the essence of
what was soon to be called "federalism" as distinct from

"republicanism." In thus binding the men of property to the national government, the states would be irreparably weakened. This was Hamilton's intention. Faced with such a prospect, the nationalist Madison saw that the future would be one of growing competition between the national and state governments, with, in his opinion, growing danger to local government and individual liberty. The delicate balance between national and local interests he had sought to establish by means of the Constitution would be upset in favor of the national. The question was whether such a "nation" was worth the risk to liberty. To Hamilton the answer was easy—the national advantage was worth almost any risk. To Madison the answer came hesitantly and reluctantly—the risk was too great.

For the rest, Hamilton's report to Congress called for a full-scale tax program, based on imposts and a long schedule of excises on "luxuries" to provide money to run the government and meet the obligations of the funded debt. Even here, the Secretary prompted a change in the political weather which was to become a violent storm four years later. Whiskey, it turned out, was not a "luxury" to the farmers of western Pennsylvania!

Finally, and almost parenthetically, Hamilton told the House he counted on a "national bank, for which, with the permission of the House, he would submit a plan in the course of the session."

It should not detract from Hamilton's stature as a national fiscal planner that there was nothing really new in this report. He was borrowing, consciously, from the British fiscal system, especially as propounded in the House of Commons by William Pitt. And, indeed, he borrowed liberally from his own earlier writings and speeches and from the papers Robert Morris had presented to the old Congress. What was new was putting the elements together into one logical whole and showing the articulation of the parts. Hamilton's mastery of the subject enabled him thus to transform hesitant, even desperate efforts of earlier years into a viable plan which the new national government he had helped to project could in fact adopt and he himself could carry out.

The second session of the first Congress was devoted almost

wholly to debate on Hamilton's report and the various bills submitted to carry it into effect. It was apparent from the outset that there would be a majority for funding and for most of the tax program. But the funding measure was in trouble because its opponents were joined by those who demanded discrimination in favor of the original holders. This was Madison's plea, and his immense prestige as a leading maker of the Constitution and a close adviser to the President led to a nearly equal division on the question. When, in addition to his powerful moral appeal for discrimination, Madison added trenchant criticism of assumption, the Hamiltonian majority disappeared.

Throughout the spring of 1790 the debate continued. On the floor of the House, Madison led the opposition, always with quiet deference to his long-time friend and collaborator, the Secretary of the Treasury. Off the floor, Hamilton himself led the federalist forces, providing fresh arguments and suggesting parliamentary tactics to prevent a vote that would defeat the bill for funding-assumption. On the five separate votes that were nevertheless taken, the Hamiltonians were each time defeated, though never by a margin large enough to be completely discouraging. And so the battle raged. Madison was establishing a reputation as champion of the common man, which laid a base both for his own later political career and for the Republican party he was, not yet consciously, helping to found. Hamilton was fighting his accustomed fight for what seemed to him sound principle and practical administration against irrational and sentimental democracy. Finally the funding portion of the plan was separated and passed and sent to the Senate in much the form Hamilton desired. But assumption appeared, by the end of June, to be hopelessly lost.

Hamilton, however, was unwilling to give up. Not only was his pride as a political leader involved, but his conviction that without assumption the whole system would fail and with its failure the best hope for a strong nation would be gone. Since he could not find the votes to rescue the plan under existing circumstances, he would have to resort to the hated game of politics—he would have to make some kind of deal. With

Madison, his leading opponent, there was no basis for negotiation. Hamilton could think of no *quid pro quo* and, in any case, Madison was too far committed.

But Hamilton thought there was just a bare possibility that it would be worthwhile to mention the problem to his new colleague, Secretary of State Thomas Jefferson, who had arrived from France and taken up his duties on March 22. Hamilton had had little opportunity to get to know Jefferson. The Virginian did not move in New York society and seemed, on the whole, disdainful of the efforts being made to turn the President's household into a court. What he really seemed to be interested in was establishing a patent office, which by law came under his department. And he had expressed, so Hamilton had heard, strong views about keeping the permanent capital of the United States away from the easy reach of the businessmen and financiers of Boston, New York and Philadelphia.

An issue had, in fact, developed among proponents of various locations for the capital, and Hamilton, who had paid scant attention to it, now noted that most of his supporters in the Congress favored a Northern or Eastern site, while his opponents favored a Southern. From his own point of view the matter was quite secondary to the fiscal and financial system. And so he approached Jefferson to sound him out on a possible deal. To his delight, Jefferson thought something might be done. Presently something *was* done which profoundly affected the whole subsequent course of American history. In exchange for Jefferson's efforts (Madison having been persuaded to go along) to secure two votes for assumption, Hamilton would provide two votes for a capital on the Potomac, while both sides would agree to a temporary, ten-year location at Philadelphia. Thus after 1800 the seat of government of the United States would be Washington; after 1790 the system of government of the United States would be Hamilton's.

The "great compromise" was carried out in the House in short order. Afterward Jefferson always contended that he had not fully understood the significance of the issue, that if he had he would not have agreed. This was not wholly candid.

Madison surely understood exactly what was at stake and Jefferson could not have been quite so ignorant of economics and finance as he claimed. The truth was that before long Jefferson and his followers came to realize that they had lost the first major engagement in a political war that was to last ten years; their regrets were understandable. As for Hamilton, he was content; he had not only won but he had given up nothing that was of real consequence in his plan of government. If Representative White of Virginia had, as Jefferson recorded years later, changed his vote on assumption "with a revulsion almost convulsive," the Secretary of the Treasury never felt better than when he persuaded a couple of New Yorkers to vote for a capital at Georgetown.

IV

Between the twenty-first of July, 1790, when the assumption bill was passed, and the return of Congress to New York in the fall, Thomas Jefferson apparently acquired a thorough education in the political consequences of economic policy. At any rate, he and Madison bent all their considerable efforts to preventing the adoption of Hamilton's proposed national bank. Thus Hamilton now found himself locked in a political struggle where no compromise or deal of any kind was possible. He had to marshal enough votes to pass the bank bill or see his whole system put in jeopardy by the state-oriented local banks, whose notes would endlessly fluctuate in value and make a rational fiscal plan nearly impossible.

This time there was a second issue which soon became paramount—the meaning of the Constitution. The power of Congress to fund the debt, even to assume state debts, had not been disputed. It had been a matter of policy. But to charter a national bank was not only to support the policy as adopted but to assume that powers not expressed in the Constitution could be implied. The debate could not be confined to fiscal and financial expediency, therefore, but involved all sorts of questions Hamilton thought irrelevant and obscurantist.

Secretary Hamilton sent his *Report on a National Bank* to

the House on December 14, 1790, "in obedience," as he put it, to the request of the House for his further recommendations as to what was "necessary for establishing the public Credit." This second of Hamilton's celebrated reports consists chiefly of a series of well-articulated propositions aimed to show the advantages to the whole nation of a nationally chartered, though privately directed, bank. He cited the examples of Italy, Germany, Holland, France and, of course, England to indicate the importance of a central bank to successful commercial, manufacturing and agricultural enterprise as well as to the efficient conduct of the public business. The principal virtues of such a bank he listed as: (1) "augmentation of the active or productive capital of a country"; (2) "greater facility to the Government in obtaining pecuniary aids, especially in sudden emergencies"; (3) "facilitating the payment of taxes." Turning to the common objections, Hamilton makes the point repeatedly that "usury" or "overtrading," etc., do in fact sometimes occur under a central banking system, but that such evils are sporadic and inconsequential contrasted with the benefits.

Without even mentioning the Constitution, Hamilton goes on to outline the charter of his proposed bank, comparing it with the Bank of North America, then operating under Pennsylvania charter but stimulated originally by the Confederation Congress. He indicates that if that bank were more efficient, he would not object to taking it over instead of starting a new bank. But on the whole the best procedure was to charter a new bank, giving it by law broad powers over credit and the issue of currency. The bank would be privately owned except that the President would be authorized to buy on behalf of the Treasury up to $2 million of stock, that is, one-fifth, since the bank was to be capitalized at $10 million. The bank was to be required to furnish the Secretary of the Treasury "as often as he may require, not exceeding once a week," full statements of the bank's accounts. The Secretary, for his part, was to have the right to inspect the books of the bank at any time.

The first reactions against Hamilton's bank were to have been expected: too much power would be placed in the hands of the rich, the state banks would lose their autonomy, small banking would be discouraged, and dubious paper transactions would replace the reliable exchange of gold and silver coins. Representatives like Fisher Ames dismissed such objections with a fine mixture of detailed refutation and disdain. But when Madison took the floor, there was a new and different story to be told.

It is probably fair to say that Madison, like Jefferson and many other republican farmers, had a prejudice against all banks, and it is certain that he feared the consequences to small farmers, merchants and "mechanics" if an institution like the Bank of England should grow up in the United States. But he feared much more the consequences of admitting that implied powers, derived by construction of the Constitution, could be used to justify such an institution. Thus when he took the floor of the House to attack the bank bill, he appealed first (February 2, 1791) to the importance of diversity to the economic system, and second (February 9) to the great question of constitutionality. "The most important of the advantages" of the proposed bank, he said, "would be better obtained by several banks, properly distributed, than by a single one." The bill would authorize the bank to establish branches, to be sure, but there could be no healthy competition since there would be only one management. There would be, in short, a banking monopoly, the worst of all possible economic evils. "The case in America," said Madison, "was different from that in England: . . . the genius of the Monarchy favored the concentration of wealth and influence at the metropolis." In a republic like the United States, the more the wealth was broken up and distributed, the better. To this the Hamiltonians could, and did, reply by reemphasizing the values of efficiency and the need for a young nation to gain strength by concentrating its economic and political resources.

And then Madison turned to the Constitution. His prestige as the principal author of the document gave his remarks, of course, a sanction no one else could command. The Constitution, he said, had been intended to strengthen the central government and to do so had certainly taken some powers from the states. But these powers had been specified and no others were included or intended. It was the enumerated powers to which the people of the states had given their consent. Among them there was no power to charter a bank; indeed, there was no power to charter anything.

He went on to list the three enumerated powers to which the proponents of the bank could sensibly appeal: power (1) to lay taxes to pay debts, and to provide for the common defense and general welfare; (2) to borrow money; and (3) to pass all laws "necessary and proper" to carry into execution the powers specified. As for the first, since no taxes were involved, the appeal must be to the "general welfare." If so, this was the most dangerous possible kind of distortion of the Constitution. On such a principle, Congress could incorporate any sort of institution its majority thought would be conducive to the general welfare—"even religious societies." If it were claimed that Congress could act so long as its acts did not interfere with the rights of the states, Madison argued that any national institution would interfere with state prerogatives; that it was the purpose of enumeration to prevent the establishment of institutions not agreed to by the states. Congress could, for example, on this specious principle, pay religious teachers "out of the Treasury of the United States, leaving other teachers unmolested in their functions." In short, on the question of the bank bill rested the far more important question whether the national government was to be one of limited powers, as had been intended, or, by construction, a government of unlimited powers.

Despite the force of Madison's argument, which Hamilton himself recognized, the Secretary was able to hold enough of his supporters in line to win a narrow victory in the House. The Senate promptly passed the bill by a large federalist margin and sent it to the President.

But the issue was by no means resolved, and Hamilton's major part was yet to be played. For Washington had been deeply impressed by Madison's argument. He had no desire to inaugurate the new government by signing legislation which violated the Constitution he had pledged himself to make a success. If the bank bill was in fact contrary to the Constitution, he would veto it, no matter how important it might be to the national economic health and stability—and he agreed with Hamilton on its importance. Thus in doubt as to what he should do, he asked the members of his Cabinet to give him their opinions in writing.

Attorney General Edmund Randolph and Secretary of State Jefferson submitted their opinions first. Both believed the bill unconstitutional. Randolph's somewhat legalistic paper has been lost to the national memory, but Jefferson's became in short order the classic expression of the so-called strict constructionist school of constitutional interpretation. Like Madison, he insisted that the Constitution grants only limited and enumerated powers to Congress. Since none of these authorizes the chartering of a bank explicitly, the only alternative is to interpret one or more articles to cover it. The only such article available would be the welfare clause. But this clause is tied to the power to tax. The taxing power, Jefferson wrote, was granted in order to do three things: (1) pay the debts, (2) provide for the common defense, and (3) promote the general welfare. The welfare clause cannot be separated from the taxing clause. There is no grant of power simply to promote the general welfare. To imply such a grant, he said, "would reduce the whole instrument to a single phrase, that of instituting a Congress with power to do whatever would be good for the United States; and, as they would be the sole judges of the good or evil, it would be also a power to do what evil they please."

There could be no disputing the force of Jefferson's argument. Together with Randolph's opinion (Washington had great confidence in this able Virginian's judgment) and Madison's speeches in the House, it provided a formidable armament for Hamilton to bring down. At this stage, indeed, the whole issue would be resolved one way or the other by Hamilton's ability to convince the President both that the bank was necessary and that it would not open the way to unlimited or otherwise dangerous use of political power.

To his opinion on the constitutionality of the bank Alexander Hamilton gave the best and most concentrated intellectual effort of his life. Whatever he may have said in private to friends like Fisher Ames or Oliver Wolcott about the insolence of "democrats" and the impractical position of Jefferson, Hamilton well knew that he could not afford to indulge in sharp talk in a paper for Washington. He took up the matter of constitutional interpretation soberly, systematically and incisively, with the result that he secured not only a charter for a bank but a charter for the "loose construction" of the Constitution which has become in the twentieth century the principal secret of the continued success of the American system—the famous "flexibility" and "vitality" of the Constitution.

It is an engaging paradox of the American mind, in fact, that these Founding Fathers who are today so frequently celebrated for their vision and foresight in framing a Constitution viable enough to survive through even revolutionary changes, in reality did no such thing. Most of them supposed that they were writing and promulgating a tight set of rules within which the national government must forever operate—unless changed by amendment—under the jealous eyes of the still sovereign states. A few, like Gouverneur Morris and, perhaps, James Wilson, regretted but did not deny that this was what they were doing. Only Alexander Hamilton, mastering with some effort his feeling of contempt for what he thought was the cowardice of the framers in the face of public opinion, accepted the result of the Convention and fought for its adoption in the belief that the system, once set up, could be modified by statute and by executive action into something like the strong central government of his dreams. It was his program and, in 1791, his brilliant defense of the use of implied powers to set up the Bank of the United States which provided the principles of flexibility and interpretation so useful and so unquestioned today. And though he won his battle, it should not be forgotten that he lost the next phase of the long war that followed. It was Jefferson's strict construction that ruled the minds of the American majority in the nineteenth century and was applied with stern vindictiveness in later years by Andrew Jackson to crush forever the Bank of the United States. Despite contemporary vindication of the Hamiltonian view of the Constitution, the United States remains the only major power in the world without a national bank.

Hamilton states it as the purpose of his *Opinion on the Constitutionality of the Bank* "to give the utmost possible satisfaction to the mind of the President." His method was to examine one by one the objections of the Attorney General and the Secretary of State while, at the same time, adducing his own positive arguments. For example, both Randolph and Jefferson had argued that the bank bill did not involve a power to lay and collect taxes. Hamilton showed that the bank was so intimately bound up with the tax-collecting function that it could not be disentangled. The notes of the bank were to serve as a national circulating medium, one purpose of which was to enable the federal treasury to collect taxes in uniform money. Thus if Congress had a power to collect taxes and could determine what to spend the money for, it could certainly specify the medium in which it would accept tax payments. The bank, as a means to this end, could not be contrary to either the spirit or the letter of the Constitution. In fact, the process envisioned in the bank bill "serves to exemplify the natural and direct relation which may subsist between the institution of a bank and the collection of taxes."

Again, the Constitution specifies that Congress shall have power to make "all needful rules and regulations respecting the Territory or other Property of the United States" (IV, 3). Is not the money of the United States as much its property as land? If so, how can it be unconstitutional to make rules governing its collection, or borrowing it, or otherwise disposing of it, for example, by investing it in a national bank?

As these examples show, Hamilton's method was not so much to try to add constructive powers to those specified as to argue that what was already specified included what was proposed in the bank bill. Thus he did not argue against the prime contention that the grants of power were enumerated only; rather he accepted that premise. He, too, was for a government of limited powers. The point he was urging on Washington was that the enumerated powers must not be so narrowly interpreted as to render them nugatory.

Thus if Congress could establish an institution for one

specified purpose—erect, say, a government in the Western territories—it could establish another institution—a bank—to expedite the collection of taxes. Granted it could only tax for the general welfare, as Jefferson had said; but taxing to raise money for investment in a national bank was precisely for the promotion of the general welfare. The point of the welfare clause was not to prevent spending public money for purposes Congress judged in the general interest, but to guarantee that the public money would be so spent. "The arguments for or against a measure in this light," he wrote, "must be arguments concerning expediency or inexpediency not constitutional rights."

One of the most interesting points in Hamilton's paper, in the perspective of later developments in the long struggle over national banking, was his suggestion that Congress, as an alternative to chartering a national bank, might order that bills (paper money) "be issued under the direction of certain officers, payable on demand," and might then set up a fund for the purpose. It could also set up a "place for the safe-keeping of such funds." But this procedure would amount to establishing a bank, as would immediately become obvious if people other than government officers were allowed to deposit their moneys at that place. From this Hamilton drew the conclusion that Congress could just as well charter an actual bank for the same purpose. More than fifty years later, President Polk temporarily resolved the national bank question by proposing and putting through Congress exactly such a "subtreasury." Thus the last of the great Jeffersonians, conscious only of his devotion to "strict construction," agreed with Alexander Hamilton as to what was "constitutional." The pleasant irony is that Polk called his creation "the constitutional treasury"!

Washington, after due meditation, declared himself satisfied by Hamilton's analysis of the issue. He signed the bill, and the Bank of the United States came into being. With this achievement Hamilton reached the height of his power. And that, to be candid, was the trouble. To the faction developing in opposition to his economic policy, it was certainly the growth of the Secretary's power, backed both by the men of private wealth and by the national government, that excited their opposition. It was not so much his measures as their usefulness as means to his power—and the bogey of a hated "monarchy" —that concerted the political efforts of the anti-federalists. Hamilton, for his part, was not afraid to fight for his principles—or for his power.

Chapter 4

A NATION-BUILDER BECOMES
A PARTY-BUILDER

I

How rapidly the political situation at the American capital (now in Philadelphia) deteriorated in 1791 is illustrated by the fact that in January, before the bank fight in the Cabinet, Hamilton and Jefferson were signing their notes and letters to each other "affectionately" or "with affection and respect." Yet by June, Jefferson and Madison were making their fateful "botanizing trip" that took them to Albany and the eventual alliance between the Clintons, the Livingstons and the Virginians, between the democracy of New York and that of the Old Dominion, which was to become the Democratic party. Alexander Hamilton, for his part, had decided to subsidize John Fenno's paper, the *Gazette of the United States* (which was moved to Philadelphia), in part no doubt because he needed a printer for Treasury business, but in part also to make sure that a paper devoted to his principles and his personal leadership would be financially secure. Jefferson and Madison countered by bringing the Revolutionary poet Philip Freneau to Philadelphia as translator and printer for the State Department and editor of a new newspaper called *The National Gazette*. That Freneau's paper proceeded to laud the Secretary of State and criticize the Hamiltonian system and its creator came as a surprise to nobody.

Beneath the surface of most profound political controversies are to be found, if one takes the trouble to put aside prejudices and allegiances, not only differences of interest but some fundamental difference in philosophy. And so it was in the bitterly partisan struggles which nearly destroyed the

United States in the 1790s. There is always a temptation to oversimplify a complex problem in politics, as elsewhere, and it is necessary to remember that the issues between the Hamiltonians and the Jeffersonians, soon to be known as Federalists and Republicans, were indeed complex. But there is one especially useful key to understanding them—the meaning of the term "corruption." Hamilton, like most political philosophers of earlier times, believed that self-interest governs the actions of men, so that successful government will make its prime appeal to self-interest. "What's in it for me?" is an ancient and recurring question. Hamilton's system of government undertook to answer that question by saying, in effect, to the men of property and capital: "Security for your holdings and contracts and growing prosperity will be your reward for identifying your interest with the national government."

But having said as much, he was not willing to leave the matter in the realm of words. The system had to prove itself to these people to whom it was appealing. Thus Hamilton very distinctly wanted the rich to get richer by buying government "stock," by investing in the national bank, by relying on the national government, not the states, to enforce contracts and maintain sound money. The rich, in Hamilton's view, would always be the powerful, and their attitude toward any government would make it or break it. If he did not in fact ever say that "the people is a great beast," as the old fable has it, he certainly did frequently give "the people" a vote of no confidence. Neither property nor contracts could be secure, in his view, if government had to act on the whim of simple, changeable majorities. The poor and uneducated were not wise enough to know their own true interest and could easily be led by demagogues to suppose that their poverty and ignorance were caused by the rich and well-born. The truth, as he saw it, was that the one best hope for broader prosperity and rising standards of educational and cultural achievement lay in the continuing prosperity of the rich, whose wealth would create jobs and markets to the advantage of everybody.

At what point, under such a system, would intentional catering to the self-interest of the rich become corruption? Almost before his program had been adopted, Hamilton was faced with a specific case. He had appointed his old friend William Duer, New York financier, as Assistant Secretary of the Treasury, confident that Duer's involvement in the financial community would help to involve the financial community in the government. And so it did! Duer quietly passed the word that the debts of the nation and of the states were to be funded at par, thus encouraging his friends to buy them up cheap wherever they could find them. This was the beginning of the storm of speculation that nearly brought down Hamilton's painfully constructed edifice. And Duer bought heavily himself. When the funding bills became law, not only the private financiers but Duer himself took immense profits. Duer's position presently became scandalous and he was forced to resign. His case, at the very beginning of American national government, well illustrates a continuing problem that government has never been able to resolve. What is a conflict of interest and how may one be avoided?

One answer, then and now, is for a government official, upon taking office, to divest himself of business investments that might be improved by his official actions. Hamilton sold his holdings in the Bank of New York before becoming Secretary of the Treasury; Robert McNamara, in the 1960s, sold his stock in the Ford Motor Company before becoming Secretary of Defense. Hamilton, clearly, saw a potential conflict of interest in his own case. Why, then, did he permit his assistant not only to keep his bank stocks but to speculate in the very government securities he was helping to manage? Hamilton certainly knew what was happening, yet he took no action until Duer's activities were exposed as contrary to the funding law itself. Personal friendship may have had something to do with it, but it seems reasonable to suppose that the role Duer was playing on behalf of the Treasury had a good deal more influence on Hamilton's judgment. If making money out of his job was, in effect, Duer's price for serving the Treasury and bringing along the moneyed men of New York—and Boston and Philadelphia—Hamilton seems to have felt that it was worth it. The stakes were no less than the future credit and stability of the United States. Since human beings were guided by self-interest anyway, the practical view of the matter would be to overlook a certain crassness on the part of his assistant while the self-interest of the men who mattered was being attached to the Treasury. In after years Jefferson characterized Hamilton's position in these words: "honest as a man, but, as a politician, believing in the necessity of either force or corruption to govern men." This was a fair statement which Hamilton himself might have accepted, only perhaps shying away from the word "corruption."

But in 1791, what was practical self-interest to Hamilton was corruption to his opponents. Above all, it was anathema to the farmers and city workers, who either owned no property at all or were land poor. And they had good cause. Hamilton was interested in liquid capital. Only money, or what could be used for money in commercial and financial transactions, could, he believed, fructify the American economy. He was no enemy of agriculture, but he did intentionally leave the farmers out of his plans for building the nation. He sought a balance of commerce, manufactures and agriculture, but it was the former two elements which were in need of government assistance and which were in a position to aid the government. An underdeveloped country, then as now, could not be developed without capital, and capital was not to be obtained from farmers except as increasing supplies of money made tax collections richer. The farmers, for their part, felt the discrimination that was taking place and resented it. Thomas Jefferson not only saw what was happening and, as a farmer, opposed it; he saw also that the vision of an agrarian democratic republic was withering away and being replaced by an aristocratic republic of urban wealth.

Hamilton had not traveled abroad. His knowledge of the great powers of Europe was derived from reading and from conversations with Europeans visiting in America. What impressed him was the power that a nation with a sound fiscal and adminstrative system could wield among nations. He wanted that power for his own country. Jefferson, in contrast, had lived for years in France and traveled widely over Europe. Everywhere he had been impressed by the majesty of cities and the poverty of the countryside. But even in the cities, he had seen, behind the glittering evidences of human creative achievement, the rags and hunger of the countless poor. In France he had seen the Revolution coming because of this vital contradiction, and had played an important part in advising its early leaders. Cities, he had come to believe, were doomed to blight. Only a strong yeomanry, citizen farmers owning their own land and prospering on it, could make republican liberty a reality. He often contrasted what seemed to him the corruption of the rich in Europe with the virtues of the farmers at home. He was no Rousseauist, no believer in the natural goodness of man, but he was certain that there was a solid measure of goodness in man's nature which could come to the fore only if he was free and self-respecting. Hamilton, it seemed to him, was not only working toward a European model of great cities with inevitable rural decline, but using corruption as a tool to his purpose.

II

Whether, on their visit to Albany, Jefferson and Madison had talked seriously with Clinton about possible political collaboration to stop the drift toward what they saw as monarchical centralization, or had merely speculated on what might be the meaning of events for dedicated republicans, it is certain they were not reassured by the message Hamilton sent to Congress when it reconvened in the fall. And the men of the land saw their fears confirmed: the Secretary's newest proposal was nothing less than a full-scale program of federal aid to industry to encourage the growth of domestic manufactures. The cost to agriculture was immediately obvious.

Hamilton's *Report on Manufactures,* sent to Congress December 5, 1791, was both the most ambitious and the most radical of his great contributions to the building of the American nation. Though it is easy to exaggerate the degree to which the document anticipated the actual trends of American economic development, it is nevertheless sure evidence of Hamilton's remarkable foresight. As a prophet in the economic field he was at least as successful as was Jefferson in the political. Fortunately neither man turned out to be right when he invaded the other's proper province. It would be disquieting, at the least, to imagine a United States in the twentieth century governed by Hamilton's political vision and Jefferson's economic daydreams!

Taking an opportunity afforded him almost two years earlier, to recommend to Congress measures "for the encouragement and promotion of such manufactories as will tend to render the United States independent of other nations for essential, particularly for military supplies," Hamilton presented a sketch of an industrial and commercial society. Much of what he wrote belongs to the theory of political economy and will be treated in Chapter VII. Here it will be enough to summarize his reasons for promoting an industrial economy and his recommendations for doing so.

The principal advantages of manufactures to the United States, in Hamilton's opinion, were these:

1. The division of labor.
2. An extension of the use of machinery.
3. An additional employment to classes of the community not ordinarily engaged in the business.
4. Promoting of emigration from foreign countries.
5. Furnishing greater scope for the diversity of talents and dispositions which discriminate men from each other.
6. Affording a more ample and various field for enterprise.
7. Creating in some instances a new, and securing in all a more certain and steady demand for the surplus produce of the soil.

This imposing list, it should be understood, was commended to Congress in addition to the advantages suggested in their own request to the Secretary of the Treasury: securing independence from other countries for military and other essential supplies.

It is interesting that while the republican faction quickly challenged the last point in Hamilton's list of advantages, holding on the contrary that the relative position of agriculture would certainly be diminished, not improved, by encouraging manufactures, they took no exception to the third point, which Hamilton explained as referring to the employment of women and children. The republicans were no more ancestors of the humanitarians who sought women's rights or opposed child labor than were the federalists.

To bring these presumed advantages to reality, Hamilton made eleven detailed suggestions, some of which were hardly controversial, others certain to arouse republican opposition, and all together forming a system for promoting industrialization which could place the United States eventually on a footing of competition with Europe.

The first two recommendations involved the use of the commerce power. Hamilton would levy duties upon all manufactured imports which were to be encouraged at home, i.e., establish a protective tariff scale. On some articles he would raise the tariff to a prohibitive figure in order to keep them entirely out of the American market. Thus the American manufacturer would be protected from price competition on those items which he could not produce quite so cheaply as could the Europeans, and given immunity from competition, at least for a time, on those items which he had not previously produced at all. This tariff system would help the manufacturer at the expense of the farmer, at least at the outset, since it was the farmer whose economic livelihood depended on exchanging raw materials for the finished goods of Europe. Forced to buy domestic manufactures, the prices he had to pay would go up and so he would be effectively subsidizing the very market in which he bought. From his point of view, low tariffs or none at all were desirable. The debate which Hamilton's tariff policy brought on has never been entirely resolved, and in the nineteenth century especially was often the chief issue between the political parties.

Another suggestion made by the Secretary of the Treasury was to prohibit the export of materials needed by manufacturers. This was in line with the mercantilist system practiced by the British as well as some other European countries, and in sharp conflict with the laissez-faire system then being advocated by Adam Smith and other economists. But Hamilton was building a nation, not projecting an international economic utopia. Again, however, his plan tended to hurt the farmer, who would now be forced to sell his fibers in a domestic market where the price might well be less than Europe was paying.

The fourth and fifth proposals were to pay "bounties" to manufacturers out of tariff revenues to encourage greater production, and to pay "premiums" to selected manufacturers who might produce an especially fine product or solve an important technical problem of production that would benefit the nation. Yet again the advantage to manufacturers would be at the expense of agriculture, since farmers were the principal importers of manufactured goods and it was their money principally that would pay the tariff.

At the same time, Hamilton proposed that manufacturers should be able to import the materials they needed in their business either duty free or with substantial "drawbacks" on the tariff, thus directly discriminating to the advantage of the manufacturer as against the farmer.

One noncontroversial recommendation had already been enthusiastically made by Jefferson. This was to provide "pecuniary rewards and, for a time, exclusive privileges" to inventors whose inventions were beneficial to industry. As Secretary of State, Jefferson had already showed more interest in the Patent Office than in foreign policy; he could be counted on to support Hamilton in this element of his plan if not in others.

Finally, Hamilton proposed that manufacturing establishments and products be carefully inspected by the federal government to make sure that high standards were maintained and that there was continuing progress, and that Congress take measures wherever necessary to facilitate the transportation of commodities. On the latter point it is rather surprising that Hamilton contented himself with a quotation from Adam Smith's *The Wealth of Nations* on the advantages of "good roads, canals, and navigable rivers." One would think that the vital importance of the transportation system to his whole program for the nation would have led him to projecting a detailed proposal in that field. But he never did so, and it was more than ten years later (in the administration of Jefferson!) that another Secretary of the Treasury, Albert Gallatin, offered to Congress the first overall plan for internal improvements.

But even without such a plan in a field which was later on to raise vital constitutional issues, Hamilton had included quite enough matters of controversy in his *Report on Manufactures.* That there would be a constitutional objection he anticipated in his discussion of bounties and premiums. He was careful not to go again into the matter of implication—the bank fight had taught him a lesson. Instead, he insisted that payments from the Treasury to businessmen were for the "general welfare," as that phrase was intended in I, 8 of the Constitution. "The only qualification of the generality of the Phrase," he wrote, "which seems to be admissible, is this—That the object to which an appropriation of money is to be made be *General,* and not *local.*" That is, it should affect everyone's welfare, "in fact, or by possibility, throughout the Union, and not . . . confined to a particular spot." More important, he told Congress that "no objection ought to arise to this construction that it would imply a power to do whatever else should appear to Congress conducive to the General Welfare." Taking the line of the strict constructionists, Hamilton argued that "a power to appropriate money with this latitude, which is granted too *in express terms,* would not carry a power to do any other things not authorized in the Constitution, either expressly or by fair construction." Thus Hamilton hoped to seal his plan for subsidizing manufactures against constitutional attack.

On the whole he succeeded. Madison, indeed, told Jefferson that when he had asked in the Convention who would be the final arbiter of constitutional issues, he had not expected the answer to be "Alexander Hamilton." But the Federalists were able to get much of the plan written into law without so prolonged a fight as there had been in the case of the bank.

To Hamilton's disgust, however, neither Federalists nor Republicans in Congress were much interested in his subsidy program. Manufacturers as such were, of course, happy with the subsidy idea, but many businessmen were also shipowners or otherwise engaged primarily in foreign commerce; to them the subsidy of domestic manufactures had no appeal at all, and they found themselves lining up with farmers in opposition. Since the representatives of this coalition in Congress made up the overwhelming majority, the subsidy plan, except for whale and cod fisheries, had to wait for a crisis, when, for example, shipbuilders would be paid for expanding the merchant marine. Instead, Congress enacted a whole schedule of tariffs much as Hamilton had recommended. Madison, who had himself proposed a schedule of discriminating duties, was less effective than usual in the House debates on the subject; and the Republicans had to take their defeat despite their now full-blown conviction that the Secretary of the Treasury was bent on wrecking the republic by legislation that would transform it somehow into a monarchy.

III

Hamilton himself, in a noteworthy conflict of interest which seemed not to bother him at all, presently entered into the field of manufacturing. He was careful not to invest his own money, but he not only lent his prestige to a grand manufacturing scheme but worked out its charter and program personally. At about the same time as he drew up his *Report on Manufactures,* he fostered the Society for Useful Manufactures (S.U.M.), a New Jersey corporation, and actively sought investors. Among other things, he promised his old friends at the Bank of New York that their bank could continue as a depository for the United States Treasury, a matter of great importance to the bank, at the same time suggesting that they invest in the S.U.M. Here was a first-rate example of what the Republicans considered corruption. Yet no law was broken, and men of wealth, at least, took the whole thing in stride. Hamilton was a government servant, of course, and if he talked the language of business, it was an acceptable language and the S.U.M. would make a major contribution to a national industrial potential. As for the Bank of New York, it would, with pleasure, safeguard the funds of the Treasury!

Hamilton's S.U.M. was no minor example of the Secretary's capacity for building organizations. He chose a point in New Jersey where the best roads would provide generally easy access to both New York and Philadelphia, and where water power was readily available. The corporation would be on a large scale, capitalized, in fact, at one million dollars, which was somewhat more than the total capitalized value of existing American plants. Some of the money would go to import machines and skilled workmen. Common labor would be plentiful because the site was in a well-populated area. Hamilton sold the idea to Governor William Paterson, who persuaded the New Jersey legislature to charter the company, and, for his pains, was thereafter rewarded by seeing the town named after him.

Like most of Hamilton's economic measures, public and private, the S.U.M. became an object of speculation. Among the heavy investors was William Duer, Hamilton's ex-assistant, who seemed unable to resist any opportunity to put out money for easy profits. Unfortunately for S.U.M., Duer's personal financial bubble burst just as the new industrial complex was getting its start. Duer was not only the most piratical speculator who trailed after Hamilton, but he was probably the most foolish as well as the most dramatic. His accounts at the Treasury had turned out to be more than $200,000 short when he resigned. Hamilton gave him time to make it up, but he now "lost" a substantial sum of the S.U.M. money entrusted to him and was no longer able to manage his debts. Going into bankruptcy, he finally was jailed for failure to meet his obligations. Hamilton wrote to him, not unkindly considering the series of disasters to the national economy he had brought on by his unscrupulous business conduct. "I will not now pain you with any wise remarks," said Hamilton, "though if you recover the present stroke, I shall take great liberties with you." Duer, however, did not recover and so never received the blast his long-suffering friend was preparing for him.

Loftily ignoring his own share of responsibility for the wild speculation and the crash that seemed certain to follow—and did—Hamilton lashed out at the speculators in 1792:

This time there should be a line of separation between honest Men and knaves, between respectable Stockholders and dealers in the funds, and mere unprincipled Gamblers. . . . The relaxations in a just System of thinking which have been produced by an excess of the Spirit of Speculation must be corrected. And Contempt and Neglect must attend those who manifest that they have no principles but to get money.

While the Secretary's anger and mortification are understandable, it is difficult to reconcile the stern morality of this outburst with the tough, realistic attitude which had led him to build his whole system on precisely the cupidity of mankind he now deplored. In any case, he was not prepared to change his mind about what was good for the United States. Duer and some others might have to go to jail, but the funding system and the progress toward industrialization would survive.

The bursting of the speculative bubble in 1792, of which Duer's collapse was only the most spectacular example, persuaded the Republicans that some sort of drastic action must be taken to alter, or at least check, the Hamiltonian course. The Congressional election afforded the only practical opportunity. Jefferson and Madison, supported by Freneau's *National Gazette* and an expanding anti-Federalist press, worked for the election of Republican members of the House in as many districts as they could hope to influence. Since senators were chosen by state legislatures and only one-third of them were to be elected, it was in most cases hopeless to swing enough strength to be effective. But the whole complexion of the House could be changed, they believed, if enough people were alerted to the danger.

As for the President, he seemed unwilling to take Republican advice on any of the major questions before the country. Jefferson, sitting in Cabinet, seethed inwardly as he watched the Secretary of the Treasury control national policy. Madison was seldom called upon even to give an opinion. Under the circumstances the Republicans decided to try to give Washington a jolt. There could not, of course, be any question of opposing him for reelection. Indeed, at least some of the Republican leaders did not yet despair of winning the President to their point of view. In any case, his popularity was so immense and so necessary to the still somewhat shaky new republic that even those who were disappointed by his acceptance of the Hamiltonian system had no wish to replace him.

But the Vice-President was not similarly immune to political attack. John Adams was not a popular man. His patriotism was fully recognized and his long service appreciated: these were the only reasons for his having been chosen Vice-President. But other men also had served long and patriotically, and to run one of them against Adams would not be impractical. In fact, it might be the best way to serve notice upon Washington, and the rest of the government, that Federalism was not the way the national majority wanted to go. Since President and Vice-President were at that time elected separately, one could vote for Washington but at the same time prefer a Republican for Vice-President. Should a Republican be elected, or even give Adams a good run, there might well be a change in the political climate.

The most likely candidate, in the view of Jefferson and Madison, was Hamilton's fellow New Yorker and bitter political opponent, Governor George Clinton. Clinton, well-known Revolutionary patriot, could be expected to carry his own state against Adams and to catch most of the anti-Federalist vote elsewhere. It was not a simple matter, however, to obtain anti-Federalist agreement on support of Clinton. In many states the feeling persisted that the Vice-Presidency was a matter of prestige without political significance. Thus the point of a change was easily missed. In New York the anti-Federalists were beginnng to come together in a Republican party, and with the emergence of the party came rivalry for leadership. The Clintons and Livingstons were upstaters who were not overly strong downstate. Political control of New York City, in fact, was already the prime objective in the early stages of the twelve-year struggle between Alexander Hamilton and Aaron Burr.

Burr, who had served for a time with Hamilton on Washington's staff in the Revolution and made a distinguished record as a soldier, was on good terms with Hamilton personally. But his ambition led him more and more into political opposition. Like Hamilton, Burr was a handsome man with abundant qualities of leadership; unlike Hamilton, he had no deep dedication to a set of political principles. He was "for or against nothing but as it suits his interest or ambition," as Hamilton characterized him. At any rate, Burr was free to maneuver for advantageous position in almost any political controversy that might arise, and did so as a matter of course. It is likely that by the summer of 1792 he sensed the growing popular support for Jefferson and decided, tentatively, to attach himself to the Jeffersonian faction. At the same time, however, he had no wish to let Republican activity put him behind the Clintonians in a line of succession in New York. He was already building a political base by converting a social club—Tammany Hall—into a political organization. His price, finally, for going along with the Clinton candidacy (he even threatened to run against Clinton for governor) was a free hand among New York City anti-Federalists in building the Republican party. When his price was paid, as it presently was, he worked loyally for the Jeffersonian cause—and parlayed his position into a successful run for the Vice-Presidency eight years later.

As for Hamilton, he soon had reliable reports on what was going on in New York and elsewhere. He had no choice but to support Adams as strongly as possible. Whereas in 1788 he had somewhat hesitantly attempted to keep Adams out of office, in 1792 he discovered that the Vice-President was "a real friend to genuine liberty, order and stable government." In this he was correct, though it no doubt pained him to say so. In letters to Congressional friends and businessmen in various parts of the country, Hamilton sent word of the danger that the anti-Federalists might make serious trouble for "order and stable government" if Clinton beat out Adams. Jefferson, he said, "seated on his pivot chair, and involved in all the obscurity of political mystery and deception . . . with the aid of his active tools, circulates his poison thro' the medium of the *National Gazette*." It is unlikely that Hamilton actually preached to any except the converted, but his influence may have stimulated greater effort on their part than would otherwise have been exerted. Adams, of course, was reelected. But Clinton got 50 votes to Adams' 77, while four electors voted for Jefferson, who was emphatically not a candidate, and one voted for Burr. Thus there was a total of 55 Republican votes, a substantial showing whose significance could not be missed in the face of Washington's unanimous reelection as President. Hamilton and his friends had won again, but their margin was smaller than ever, and the Federalist majority in the House was gone. Nor were they again to command a great enough majority to develop further the Hamiltonian system. The next victories of the Secretary of the Treasury were to be won, surprisingly, in the field of foreign affairs.

IV

The talents of General Washington are greatly overrated in the world. His public reputation has hitherto been supported by reserve, caution, temper, firmness, and a plain understanding, with a good choice of men around him; his present high station has lately become extremely embarrassing from a difference in the political opinion of the officers at the head of the executive departments, which affects more or less every measure of this government. If the concerns of the States, were transacted in a cabinet, the chief magistrate would be compelled to a choice, the one influence or the other would obtain a complete ascendancy; but as the President by the Constitution, can do wrong, may be impeached, and (although he practices it) is not under the necessity of demanding the opinions of the heads of departments . . . the condition of things . . . does not press to such an extremity, and he balances amidst discordant advice, sometimes leaning to one party, and occasionally to the other. The great point of difference is on an English and a French connexion; the gentleman at the head of the former, conceives the best interests of this country will be greatly promoted by a solid and permanent friendship with Great Britain, and in this opinion he is supported by the most enlightened men in the legislature; this party think that the condition of the two Countries is such as renders the formation of a commercial treaty very practicable and to the benefit of both nations and they are extremely desirous to promote it: Mr. Jefferson . . . is at the head of the latter, he is blindly devoted to a French influence, which he does not take common pains to conceal and there are no lengths in his power to which he will not go to favor the interests of that kingdom.

This contemporary summing up of the political condition of the United States government in 1791 is shrewd and largely accurate. Jefferson, of course, was not "blindly devoted" to anything, except, perhaps, individual human freedom. But the observer can be forgiven the exaggeration when one considers that he was an Englishman. The passage takes on a dimension of importance because it was contained in a report to the British Foreign Office by its secret agent in America, George Beckwith. It becomes even more interesting when one knows that Beckwith had been in close and even intimate contact since October, 1789, with the man he refers to as the head of the "English" party—Alexander Hamilton.

When Beckwith, agent of Lord Dorchester, the Governor General of Canada, arrived in New York in October, 1789, the new American government was in process of formation. It had no Secretary of State and was, in fact, paying little attention to foreign affairs. Washington had written to Jefferson, then Minister in Paris, asking him to head the Department of State as first officer of the Cabinet, but it would be months before Jefferson reached New York. Beckwith, ostensibly a visitor, took every opportunity to learn what he could about the sentiments of the men who were to play leading parts in Washington's administration and to cultivate those who might be kindly disposed toward England. He called on the new Secretary of the Treasury immediately—and immediately found what he wanted. The two men had so strong a common interest that Hamilton was certainly indiscreet in conversation and presumptuous in the undertakings he gave the Englishman. In the light of twentieth-century hindsight, indeed, Hamilton, coded by Beckwith as "7," appears almost to have conspired to direct the foreign policy of the United

States in ways the British government would approve regardless of the wishes of Washington or, later, Jefferson.*

But in the perspective of the actual conditions in New York and Philadelphia in 1789–91, the uncertain, fledgling status of the American government, and the lack of a settled American policy, Hamilton's behavior seems to have been rash at times and interfering at others but not quite disloyal or conspiratorial. It should be remembered that his relation with Beckwith was formed long before Jefferson's return from France, at a time when he had fully as much reason to talk foreign policy as any member of the government except, of course, Washington. That he sometimes *did not report* his conversations to the President or the Secretary of State is perhaps less important than that he sometimes *did make reports* in which Beckwith was made to say what Hamilton wished him to say rather than, in every case, what he actually did say in his reports to the Foreign Office. As for Beckwith's status as a secret agent, this was no more than to say that he had no diplomatic credentials. His agency was an open secret.

Nevertheless, Hamilton certainly did see his plan for a developing and prosperous United States as crucially dependent upon close commercial and political relations with Great Britain. If he sometimes pursued his effort to bring about such relations in unacceptable ways, it is fair to say, again, that he had nothing personal to gain other than the satisfaction of seeing his program succeed. This, of course, was not the way Jefferson saw the matter.

Jefferson's idea of wise policy for the United States was greatly influenced, of course, by his experience in Europe. He had been treated coolly in England—which should not have surprised the author of the Declaration of Independence! And he had been lionized in Paris by the Revolutionary party and by intellectuals generally. The future of freedom lay, he believed, in the new thrust of the French, not the stand-pattism

* For this interpretation, heavily documented, see Julian Boyd, *Number 7: Alexander Hamilton's Secret Attempts to Control American Foreign Policy* (Princeton: Princeton University Press, 1964).

of the British. Upon taking up his duties in New York, he told the Cabinet that he was certain the Revolutionary government in France would succeed, that it would head a new European system of trade, and that from France herself and her leadership the United States could expect important commercial gains. He strongly advocated a policy of avoiding political ties with any of the great powers, only honoring the existing treaty with France, while seeking beneficial commercial relations with all nations. He was not opposed to a treaty with Great Britain, but wished to put all commercial treaties on the basis of reciprocity.

The very next day Hamilton reported Jefferson's views privately to Beckwith and frankly indicated his own disagreement with them. He favored exchanging ministers with England and entering into a commercial treaty which would go as far as England's mercantilist Navigation Acts would permit. This would mean great concessions to the British. Hamilton hoped, in fact, for no more than that small American ships might be allowed into the West Indies trade. He had been upset, apparently, by Jefferson's views and was uncertain how he should treat the position of the new Secretary of State. "I cannot at this moment," he told Beckwith, "determine whether it may be proper to communicate further with Lord Dorchester, or to carry it forward through a regular channel. Mr. Jefferson arrived last night, and these matters are in his department." A few days later, Beckwith, about to leave New York for Canada, gave Hamilton a somewhat painful hint. "I take it for granted," he said, "the different communications you have been pleased to make to me, flow from that source, which under your present Government, is alone competent to make them." Hamilton knew very well what his friend meant, but he could not answer easily. If he disclaimed authority, his position would be seriously if not fatally weakened and his hopes for rapprochement with Great Britain would be diminished. But if he claimed to speak officially, he would be telling an untruth. "I am not authorized," he finally said, "to say to you in so many words that such is the language of the President of the United States; to a gentleman, who has no public character such a declaration cannot be made [as to exchange of ministers and a commercial treaty with Great Britain], but my honor and character stand implicated in the fulfillment of these assurances." That was in April, 1790. Thus did the Secretary of the Treasury commit his personal honor to bringing about an American foreign policy contrary to that of the Secretary of State.

And he succeeded. It took time and the march of events. But by 1794 Jefferson had left the government in disgust, while Hamilton, triumphant once more—and finally—saw John Jay dispatched to London to negotiate with the British. Jefferson's policy had been defeated by a combination of the French Terror and Hamilton's politics.

For two years nothing much happened to advance American-British relations. Gouverneur Morris went to London as United States Minister, and agent Beckwith was replaced in Philadelphia by a British minister, George Hammond. But despite Hamilton's efforts in the Cabinet and among congressmen—and his unforgivable reporting to Hammond—Washington had not yet decided to move toward "an English connexion." Intrigue was the order of the day, accompanied by shrill denunciation in the press of Hamiltonians as Anglophiles and Jeffersonians as Francophiles. Such was the state of affairs when war broke out between England and France in 1793, posing an immediate need for decision by the United States.

Under the Treaty of Paris of 1778, France could call upon the United States for military assistance if she wished to do so. However, since that would mean a naval war against Great Britain, for which the United States was wholly unprepared, neither France nor the United States wished this to happen. The interest of the United States, as Washington, Jefferson and Hamilton unanimously saw it, was to maintain strict neutrality while trying to maintain profitable commercial relations with both belligerents, as the law of nations had always sanctioned.

But to agree on a policy of neutrality was not the same thing as agreeing on whether to announce it. On this issue Hamilton could speak openly since his opinion was invited by the President. To the objection that a proclamation of neu-

trality by the President would constitute, in effect, a renuncia-
tion of the treaty with France, Hamilton argued at length that
the treaty was already void or, at the least, subject to repudia-
tion by the United States. The point was, as he saw it, that the
treaty of 1778 had been contracted with the French monarchy, whereas the French Revolution had destroyed the monarchy and wholly altered the state of diplomatic affairs.
France was now a republic, so called, and was showing signs
of hostility to the United States by interfering with her
commerce. Hamilton laid down the principle he would follow
under such circumstances:

> If, then, a nation thinks fit to make changes in its govern-
> ment, which render treaties that before subsisted between
> it and another nation useless, or dangerous, or hurtful to
> that other nation, it is a plain dictate of reason, that the
> latter will have a right to renounce those treaties; because
> *it* also has a right to take care of its own happiness, and
> cannot be obliged to suffer this to be impaired by the
> means which its neighbor or ally may have adopted for
> its own advantage, contrary to the ancient state of things.

Hamilton was not at his best in this argument. His new
doctrine was consistent neither with the law of nations nor
with his own belief in the sanctity of contracts. That he was
aware of the anarchic implications of his position has to be
assumed. The importance of a neutrality proclamation to dis-
entangle the United States from France, with its subversive
Revolutionary doctrines, and to keep alive the option of closer
ties with Great Britain, evidently weighed more heavily with
Hamilton than consistency.

He was on surer ground in disputing Jefferson's contention
that the President had no constitutional power to issue a
proclamation of neutrality. If the President could say "we shall
be neutral," then he could say "we shall not be," thus usurping
the prerogative of Congress to declare war; so Jefferson
asserted. Hamilton's reply was that the President was charged
by the Constitution with the conduct of foreign relations, not
the Congress. The President could thus adopt and announce

any policy he chose, excepting only a declaration of war. If the President were limited by strained construction of the war power, he could not effectively conduct foreign policy at all.

Washington sided with Hamilton, and the proclamation—written by Jefferson!—was issued on April 22, 1793. In the light of history it is fair to give Hamilton full credit for helping to establish an interpretaton of the President's powers which might once have been optional but has since become necessary. In 1793, however, the proclamation by no means ended the foreign policy controversy. And the nation would have been in better shape if Hamilton had won the next round as well. But he lost it.

On April 8, there had arrived at Charleston the new Minister Plenipotentiary of the Republic of France, Citizen Edmond Genêt. The President now had to decide whether to receive him. Should he do so, Hamilton argued, he would appear to be endorsing the Terror and the French cause in the war. Should he not do so, Jefferson argued, he would be offering a calculated offense to the Revolutionary republic, which, despite its unfortunate excesses, was a beacon of liberty to the peoples of Europe and the long-time friend and ally of the United States. To the disgust of the President and the Secretary of the Treasury and the nervous apprehension of the Secretary of State, Citizen Genêt made his way toward Philadelphia in a kind of triumphal procession. On every possible occasion he made speeches of praise of republicanism and democracy and of their American adherents, and denounced monarchy, the British and their presumed adherents in the United States. The Republican press idolized him; the Federalist press attacked him for his bad diplomatic manners and his "Jacobinism." But despite Hamilton's warnings, Washington decided to receive Genêt.

Jefferson's victory in this battle with Hamilton was costly to his own cause. On principle, of course, he was right and Hamilton was wrong. To receive an emissary is not at all to approve the conduct of his government. Recognition does not constitute endorsement. But on the specific issue Hamilton was right and Jefferson wrong. The United States demeaned itself by receiving Genêt, who took advantage of his good fortune to embarrass Jefferson and Washington beyond endurance. The story of Genêt's misconduct—fitting out armed merchantmen, bringing in British prizes, appealing to the public against Washington, etc.—is more properly a part of the biography of Thomas Jefferson than of Alexander Hamilton. Hamilton, however, made such effective use of the whole episode in his developing attack against the Republicans that it cannot be entirely skipped over.

Hamilton had already attacked Jefferson in the press in 1792 under the pseudonym "An American." Now he took up his pen again under the name of "Pacificus" and, later, "No Jacobin," to write a series of articles attacking Jefferson and the "French party" and defending the principles of American foreign policy in vigorous and telling language. "Pacificus" enraged the Republicans by putting upon the neutrality declaration precisely the interpretation they rejected. "At the present time," wrote Hamilton, "good faith does not require that the United States should put in jeopardy their essential interests, perhaps their very existence" by condoning French behavior. "It is impossible," he said, "for any well-informed or sober-minded man not to condemn the proceedings which have been stated [the French Terror and war policy] as repugnant to the rights of nations, to the true principles of liberty, to the freedom of opinion of mankind." The appeal was to the customary language of the Jeffersonians; thus the rapier found its mark. In another paper Hamilton argued convincingly that France had come to the aid of the United States during the Revolution in her own interest, not out of altruism or love of liberty. The King was no doubt "a humane and kind-hearted man." But he was dead, killed by the Terror, and the French at the moment were branding him "as a tyrant, and LaFayette as a traitor. But how can we wonder at this . . . ?" Hamilton wanted to know.

Jefferson, well knowing that these papers were coming from the pen of his rival and colleague, was anxious to have them answered. He had renounced personal participation in the pamphlet wars from the beginning, but he was never averse to encouraging others to polemical action. This time, in a tone of desperation, he called on Madison. "For God's sake, my

dear sir," he wrote, "take up your pen. Select the most strik-
ing heresies and cut him to pieces in the face of the public."
Madison dutifully tried to do so in the "Helvidius" papers. But
before he could make an impression, the Genêt affair had
come to a head. And Hamilton, as "No Jacobin," could fairly
lash out: "breaches of decorum lose their importance when
mingled with injuries and outrages."

> We read of cases [he wrote] in which one nation has
> raised men for military service in the dominions of an-
> other, with the consent of the nation in whose territories
> they were raised; but the raising of men, not only with-
> out the consent but against the will of the government of
> the country in which they are raised, is a novelty re-
> served for the present day, to display the height of
> arrogance on one side and the depth of humiliation on
> the other.

When Genêt, ordered to cease his subversive activities, tried
to appeal over Washington's head to the general public, Jefferson could no longer defend him. Washington asked for his
recall and he retreated from the public stage in disgrace.
Jefferson's cup of misery was now full, and by the end of the
year he had retired to Monticello. Randolph was appointed
Secretary of State, but Hamilton continued his interference in
matters of foreign policy. Indeed, he was more effective than
ever.

V

In domestic politics, however, things had not gone so well
for the Secretary of the Treasury in 1793. Under the shock of
the election of 1792, which had apparently returned a Republican majority to the House of Representatives, the House
voted a set of resolutions offered by William Giles of Virginia
demanding, in effect, an accounting by the Treasury. Jefferson,
lashing at Hamilton as viciously as Hamilton struck at him,
had drafted the Giles resolutions, using language so strong as
practically to demand the resignation of the Secretary of the
Treasury. The House toned them down considerably, but the

result was nevertheless annoying to Hamilton. His pride was now hurt just as he was recovering from a behind-the-scenes impugning of his honor.

It would be pleasant, no doubt, if one could say flatly that the revered Founding Fathers of the United States were always as virtuous as they were brilliant and patriotic. Few, if any of them, of course, were any such thing. Jefferson, for one, as a young man made improper advances to the wife of a friend. Alexander Hamilton, perhaps as happily married as any man of the time, allowed himself to be caught in a vulgar affair with an attractive woman who was also the partner of a blackmailing husband.

The affair with Mrs. Maria Reynolds began in 1791 and lasted about a year. Shortly after it began, Mr. Reynolds called upon Hamilton and expressed sorrow that he had been betrayed by his infatuated wife. It turned out that his wounded feelings could be assuaged by gifts of money. For a thousand dollars Reynolds agreed to leave town and not again bother the lovers. But presently he ran out of money, or so he said, and returned for more to the source he had carefully developed. For a time Hamilton apparently believed that the Reynoldses were what they seemed. By the end of 1792, however, he had not only lost interest in the lady but concluded that he was the victim of a blackmail conspiracy.

Meanwhile, Reynolds and a partner, Jacob Clingman, were arrested for fraud and jailed in Philadelphia. There they let it be known that they were in possession of evidence that would convict Treasury officials, including the Secretary, of corruption and embezzlement. This word they sent to Congressman Frederick Muhlenberg, who, joined by Congressman Abraham Venable and Senator James Monroe, all of course Republicans, called on Clingman and Reynolds in jail and heard from them a story that appeared to convict the leader of the hated "monocrats" of high crimes and misdemeanors. Into their hands, in fact, were put certain of Hamilton's letters to Reynolds that seemed to indicate the Secretary's personal involvement in corrupt speculation.

Forthwith Muhlenberg, Venable and Monroe called on Hamilton and confronted him with their evidence and the

Reynolds-Clingman story. It was a painful moment for Alexander Hamilton, the most painful of his life. If he told the truth he would hurt his wife and family; if he did not, his honor would be impeached and the whole sordid business would probably come out anyway. Under the circumstances Hamilton chose to tell the truth. To the three Republican politicians he confided the facts about his adventures with Mrs. Reynolds and the blackmail which ensued. For their part, the self-appointed—and disappointed—investigating committee accepted Hamilton's word and absolved him of any charge of dishonest dealings as a public official. They also agreed to keep the matter permanently in confidence. Oliver Wolcott was witness to their statements. And so the matter ended. At least Hamilton had reason to suppose that it had. Only some years later, under quite different circumstances, did he remember that Senator Monroe, his one-time comrade of the Revolution, had been much more restrained in his acceptance of Hamilton's story during that sickening interview than had Muhlenberg and Venable. Thereby hung a miserable tale afterward to be revealed.

Such was the state of Alexander Hamilton's personal affairs when he was called upon, in almost threatening terms, to give an accounting of his official conduct to a select committee of the House. But unpleasant as the task was, it could be done and done effectively. To the unconcealed chagrin of the Republican majority on the committee, Hamilton gave a full accounting of the nation's financial affairs. The figures might be complicated, but they were there and there were no irregularities. Later, when Albert Gallatin came into the House, it would be more difficult to dismiss Republican attacks on the Treasury system because there would be a Republican theory of finance to counter and a financial intelligence equal to his own to challenge him. But in 1793 Hamilton won an easy victory.

VI

With Jefferson gone, with the "French party" routed by the rash and unforgivable behavior of Genêt, the Washington administration had still to find an effective policy vis-à-vis the two great warring powers. Commerce with both nations was important to American prosperity; political connection with either could be disastrous. And so neutrality had been agreed upon. But American shipping was being seized or diverted on the high seas by both French and British warships, and American sailors were being impressed by the British. Decrees of both warring governments, violating the old laws of nations, in effect denied any neutral commerce with belligerent powers. The moment, in Hamilton's view, was exactly suited to a new approach to the British. Washington agreed. An effort could be made to persuade the British to evacuate the Western forts they had been holding, despite the Treaty of Paris, to wind up the claims hanging over from the Revolution, to put commerce with Great Britain on a stable basis, and to make certain the United States would not have to go to war.

Hamilton, under various pen names, kept up his fire against France and argued the advantages to the United States of neutrality and growing commerce with England. When the mission to England was decided upon, he seemed in some ways best suited to head it. There is no doubt that he hoped for the assignment. But his partisanship could too readily be held against him. Not only would the Republican faction never agree to his going, but the French government would certainly be offended. Senator Monroe, in fact, gratuitously undertook to advise the President against sending Hamilton. "I should deem such a measure," he wrote Washington, "not only injurious to the public interest, but also especially to your own." The President, through Secreary of State Randolph, rightly rejected Monroe's interference, but it was nevertheless decided that Hamilton should not go. Instead, the President appointed Chief Justice John Jay, who had been Secretary for Foreign Affairs of the Confederation. Jay was a devoted Hamilton man and a high Federalist in both national and New York politics. But he had a reputation for dispassionate judgment, and his public standing was beyond question. If he could not go himself, Hamilton could not have been better pleased by Washington's choice.

In the Senate, Monroe and six others voted against con-

firmation of Jay's appointment. Nineteen were for him, however, and he presently sailed for London, where he was to
negotiate the most demeaning international agreement to
which the United States was ever to be a party. But Jay's
weakness in negotiation was no fault of Alexander Hamilton.

Neither was the curious decision of the President to send
to Paris a well-known Republican as a kind of reassurance
that Jay's mission meant no diminution of American friendship for France. When he was consulted, Hamilton suggested
Madison, but without enthusiasm for a French mission.
Madison refused, and eventually Monroe accepted the assignment. Thus Washington sent to France an avowed enemy of
the Jay mission for the express purpose of supporting that
mission. It was only incidental to such naïveté that Monroe
was not even told that Jay's instructions, drafted by Hamilton,
included power to negotiate a commercial treaty which would
necessarily be injurious to the interests of France! The fruits
of these two ill-fated diplomatic adventures were to sicken
the young body of the United States almost to death.

VII

But long before Jay or Monroe came home, Hamilton
found himself again embroiled in violent political controversy.
As Madison and others had foretold, the tax on whiskey hit
the trans-Allegheny farmers nearly to the point of confiscation. In the summer of 1794 they rebelled. Refusing to pay
the tax any longer, several hundred farmers, against the
advice of Pennsylvania Republican leaders like Albert Gallatin, took up arms against the agents of the Treasury.
Hamilton, seeing not only a need to assert the authority of
the federal government in unmistakable terms but also an
opportunity to demonstrate that the Republicans were in fact
lawless Jacobins, called for a march into Pennsylvania by the
Army of the United States.

And there were signs, at least on the surface, that Hamil-
ton's concern was justified. In many larger cities Democratic
Clubs had been organized, chiefly to express sympathy for the
French Revolution but inevitably rallying around the name of

Jefferson. These clubs, which had been denouncing the government as monarchical and oppressive, now supported the whiskey rebels with strongly worded resolutions. The Republican press, led by Franklin's grandson, Benjamin Franklin Bache, chided the clubs and opposed the whiskey rebels in the name of law and order. But the Federalist editors gave them no credit for their loyalty. Shouting "Down with the Democratic Clubs!" and "Down with the critics of governmental measures!" Fenno's *Gazette of the United States* urged Washington and Hamilton to take drastic measures to suppress the rebellion. Washington agreed. Troops were dispatched to western Pennsylvania with the President and the Secretary of the Treasury at their head. In justification of their personal participation, it should be said that Washington wished to demonstrate his willingness to accept the Presidential role of Commander in Chief, and that Hamilton's department was involved because the rebels were rebelling against the excise laws. In Hamilton's case there can be no doubt that there were other motives. The insurrection, as was supposed, threatened the whole structure he had been seeking to build. Rampant democracy, "the mob," as he frankly called it, had to be stopped in its tracks if the nation was to survive. And he, Alexander Hamilton, had a mission to lead. From his youth in the Revolution, he had sought the glory of command. Now he had suddenly been presented with another chance.

But the rebellion fizzled out before the troops arrived; the United States Army could find no one to fight and only a few stragglers to arrest. The feelings of the President and the Secretary of the Treasury must have been a mixture of relief and exasperation. Exasperation no doubt predominated in the case of Hamilton, who insisted on rounding up the leaders and taking them to Philadelphia for trial as traitors. On reaching the Schuylkill River, the prisoners were forced to wear the inscription "INSURGENT" on their hats and were marched down Market Street like captive slaves. In the trials, however, only two men were found guilty, and Washington, his sense of proportion restored, pardoned them.

While the law was vindicated by the excessive show of federal power, the consequences of the expedition for American political life were disastrous. To the man in the street it appeared that the "best people" of Philadelphia, headed by the arrogant Hamilton, had sought out and suppressed the common men of the backwoods and hills. The aristocrats had levied war against the democrats, even if no one was hurt. Thus party lines were drawn at the extremes of the political spectrum, leaving the middle, where a stable and prosperous nation might be built, occupied by confused citizens without leaders.

In his annual message in December, Washington, reflecting the temper of the administration—and the advice of Alexander Hamilton—denounced the Democratic Clubs as "self-created societies," as though to form an organization critical of the government were a kind of treason. It was this unhappy message more than anything else that confirmed the Jeffersonians in their resolve to defeat Federalism regardless of the wishes of the President. Jefferson, in Monticello, got slowly and painfully ready to return to public life, writing dozens of letters to his fellow Republicans urging them to concentrate and redouble their efforts to bring down the Hamiltonian system.

Hamilton himself, always willing to fight for his beliefs and the power to bring them into reality, concluded that he would have to carry on the fight in private life. He needed money and, contrary to the slanderous and continuing attacks of his enemies, he could not make any in public service. Resigning his office as of January 31, 1795, he returned to New York to practice law. His language at the moment of retirement was hardly less sententious than Jefferson's had been—full of yearning for domestic tranquillity. But in New York he was closer to the scene of action than was his rival, and though he took up the law energetically, he never really "retired" from politics at all.

It would have been better for his reputation in history—and, perhaps, for the political health of his country—if he had in fact retired. At forty, he had made a record of achievement no one of his time could surpass. On any showing, he had played the foremost part in building a nation and had formed and led to victory after victory a great political party.

There had, of course, been a share of mistakes and failures, but Hamilton's admirers rightly discounted them.

VIII

In Hamilton's character pride of achievement was inextricably entangled with pride of leadership. He simply could not let go. If he disdained the notion of the indispensable man, his conduct belied him. And so he continued, behind the scenes, to dominate the Treasury through Wolcott, his handpicked successor, and through the Federalist members of Congress he sought to guide legislation. In the foreground he fought Burr and the Clintons for political control of New York. In the background he kept up a steady flow of polemical writing in the press to give signals to Federalists everywhere. His ideas were shrewd, his writings as brilliant as ever. But his moment had nevertheless passed. There were to be few achievements in the coming years, and many bitter and mostly losing battles of resistance to the steadily rising tide of republican democracy.

Chapter 5

POWER BEHIND THE THRONE

I

It would have been difficult for a humbler man than Alexander Hamilton to keep his head in the face of the adulation showered upon him by the Federalist leaders and businessmen of New York when he returned to make his home there. They gave him public and private dinners; one at the Tontine Coffee House was said to be "the most Superb ... that ever was prepared in this city." On that occasion more than three hundred people paid for the privilege of dining with Hamilton and toasting his achievements as Secretary of the Treasury. The newspapers compared him with Washington; the Bank of the United States, not surprisingly, gave him public testimonials. More important than the adulation, no doubt, was the legal business that found its way to Hamilton's office. If virtue was to be rewarded, Hamilton's refusal to make money out of public office was well repaid by retainers from men who had got rich under his system of fostering capitalism. The workers along the docks, prospering from full employment, were as enthusiastic as their bosses; one group even offered to build Hamilton a house, a gift he was politic enough to refuse.

But there were at least as many citizens of New York City whose enthusiasm was subdued or nonexistent. And presently their numbers swelled as the shocking terms of Jay's treaty became known and Alexander Hamilton was publicly identified as its unhappy defender. There was an abrupt transition from offering to build him a house to pelting him with garbage and rocks.

In his private thoughts Hamilton was almost as angry with

Jay's pusillanimous bargain as were the Jeffersonians. He had himself drafted Jay's instructions and, of course, anticipated Republican protest against any treaty that would benefit Great Britain and appear to be disadvantageous to France. To avoid war and secure a profitable commerce seemed to him well worth drawing Republican fire. Now, however, he found that his friend Jay had gone far beyond his instructions in yielding to the British; he had given much and got very little in return. Hamilton himself would never have agreed to such terms.

Because the Jay Treaty remains the most controversial ever signed by the United States, and Alexander Hamilton is forever identified with the effort to get it ratified, it will be useful to summarize its terms. Concessions by Great Britain to the United States were (1) agreement to evacuate the Western posts; (2) admission of American ships of seventy tons or less into the West Indies trade; (3) regularization of American trade with Great Britain herself and with India; and (4) establishment of mixed British-American commissions to settle territorial disputes and maritime spoliation claims. In return the United States (1) conceded that goods not contraband by the law of nations could, nevertheless, be captured from American vessels, the list including even foodstuffs, and agreed (2) not to export cotton, sugar or other products of the West Indies, (3) not to confiscate British bank deposits in the United States, (4) not to permit the fitting out of privateers in United States ports or to allow prizes to be brought in and sold. Finally, and perhaps most important, the treaty said nothing about impressment, so that the United States appeared to be yielding to the British on this sorest of all points.

The President in Philadelphia had to decide whether to sign this miserable bargain and send it to the Senate, or send it back with a demand for amendments, or to reject it outright and risk possible war with Britain. Alexander Hamilton, private citizen in New York, had to decide how to advise Washington and whether to give the treaty his public support. It was a bitter choice for both men.

For Hamilton there was a personal irony not known to the President. The previous year, after no more than a decent interval following Jay's departure, British Minister George

Hammond had called on his friend the Secretary of the Treasury to learn what instructions Jay carried with him to London. That it was none of Hammond's business apparently occurred neither to him nor to Hamilton. At any rate, Hamilton talked freely. At the earliest possible moment Hammond sent off to London a detailed account of the background of Jay's mission, what had been said in Cabinet and in private, and an exact summary of the instructions Jay had been given. Thus Lord Grenville, sitting across the table from the American Minister, knew just what limits the American government had hoped to set in making concessions. Naturally enough, Grenville negotiated as though those limits were maximum demands, and Jay was hopelessly caught without cards to play. If he nevertheless decided to go beyond his instructions, agreeing, for example, to the omission of impressment, Jay owed a part of his unhappy position to his friend Hamilton. In 1795, when the storm over the treaty broke in the United States, Hamilton knew as did no one else the handicap under which Jay had worked. He would not himself have yielded weakly as Jay had done. He might even have preferred to go to war. But how could he now repudiate Jay? Better, he finally decided, to make the best of it by putting on a bold front and attacking the enemies of the treaty, who were, after all, no better in his view than pro-French enemies of law and order.

And so Hamilton advised the President to approve the treaty and send it to the Senate for ratification. But to save American face, he suggested that Article XII, limiting American West Indies shipping to seventy-ton vessels and agreeing not to export cotton and sugar, be eliminated. This was done. On June 24, 1795, the treaty was ratified. Though the Senate voted to keep the terms secret until Great Britain had acted, the Republican Senators were so angered by the treaty and by the Federalist decision to accept it that secrecy was impossible. The text appeared in the newspapers almost immediately.

The news brought on the most violent party battle that had yet occurred, not only in Philadelphia but throughout the country. It raged for almost a year. In the forefront of the fight were Madison, Edward Livingston, Giles and Gallatin on the Republican side. Defending the treaty were Fisher Ames, Harrison Otis, the members of the Cabinet and, leading them on, Hamilton himself. The Republican line was that the British had made no concessions at all—to agree to evacuate the forts was only to agree again to do what they had agreed to do more than ten years before. Yet the Americans would now be bound to give aid and support to England in her war with France, the ally of the United States. The freedom of the seas was given up, and the right of the British not only to interdict American trade but to impress American citizens into British service was left uncontested. George III, that "hardened Pharaoh," had got revenge for the Revolution by forcing the United States into what Madison called "a ruinous bargain." The Declaration of Independence had been trod in the mud. For their part, the Federalists argued that the treaty secured the Western forts and provided suitable machinery for settling spoliation claims. Trade with England, they said, would restore American prosperity and, above all, the threat of a distastrous war had been removed.

Argument in the press was unrestrained. In coffeehouses and public meetings people often differed so violently that fighting was a common occurrence. The Republicans, said the Federalist papers, were "not afraid of a black eye or a broken head" in their efforts to prove their point. To Hamilton and his followers they did indeed prove a point—that they were lawless subversives who, like their French friends, were quite prepared to pull down the state in their irrational protests against sound policies they could not understand. Hamilton himself was considered a fair target for both verbal and actual brickbats. At a public meeting in New York, sponsored by the Republicans, Hamilton appeared to speak in defense of the treaty. There were so many hisses and catcalls that a speech was clearly out of the question; instead, he quickly introduced a motion of confidence in the President of the United States, only to have it and himself saluted with a hail of stones. Such unrestrained disgraceful behavior toward a man who had for so many years served his country brilliantly and patriotically suggests the depth of partisan feeling that Jay's treaty had brought to the surface.

But the mob spirit did not frighten Hamilton—at least not for his own safety. What did concern him was the danger of a general collapse of law and order. He sought by means of his pen to place the blame for such an imminent disaster where he was certain it belonged, and to present to all who were willing to pay attention a rational explanation of the government's problem and its reasons for approving Jay's treaty. Writing as "Camillus," the Roman leader who had saved the capital from the Gauls despite personal unpopularity, Hamilton argued the British case for impressment: "to the belligerent party it is a question of national *safety,* to the neutral party a question of commercial convenience and individual security." The concessions to British commercial policy Hamilton explained as necessary because England had long made her Navigation Acts so fundamental a part of her policy that she could not be expected to revise them to accommodate the United States. British insistence on settlement of claims against the United States, he said, was to be expected of a sovereign nation. On the other hand, American claims for damages because of British occupation of the Western forts could not be settled because there was "no satisfactory rule of compensation." Finally, to attempt to subvert the treaty was to subvert the government of the United States and to drive the country to war. No rational man would pay such a price to indulge his fondness for the French regicides.

Jefferson, reading these articles and hearing from his friends in New York and Philadelphia that Hamilton's leadership was having its effect, gave his enemy a grudging compliment. "He is really a colossus to the anti-republican party," he wrote to Madison. "Without numbers, he is an host within himself."

But as it turned out, Hamilton also had numbers, at least in the House of Representatives, where the final round of the battle was fought in the spring of 1796. The Jay Treaty came before the House, after approval by the Senate, because appropriations were needed to carry it into effect. The Republicans, led by Madison and Gallatin, made an intensive last-ditch effort to quash the treaty by denying the necessary funds. The issue, however, turned on a prior technicality which was to have enduring consequences.

This momentous side issue was the question whether the House had the right to require the Executive to produce any documents the House considered relevant to its function of appropriating money. Edward Livingston, Republican from New York, introduced a resolution asking the President to submit for the inspection of the House copies of Jay's instructions and all correspondence relating to the treaty he had negotiated except such as might be involved in continuing negotiations. The resolution was an astute ploy. If the Federalists voted for it, they would be effectively attacking the administration they wished to support. If they voted against it they would be demeaning their own branch of government. Under such pressure, many of them voted for the resolution, which was accordingly passed and forwarded to the President.

Washington was furious. The action of the House seemed to him not only arrogant in itself but to display lack of confidence in the wisdom and integrity of the President. He appealed to Hamilton for advice. Hamilton, for his part, viewed the issue both in terms of principle and in terms of the politics of the moment. In principle he knew that the Executive would be on shaky ground if he refused to hand over the papers. On the other hand, once the House saw Jay's instructions and could judge how far he had gone beyond them, Hamilton feared the treaty would be voted down. He advised Washington, therefore, that since treaties were the supreme law of the land under the Constitution (VI, 2), the House had no power to void them by use of the appropriation power. Since the House could not function to pass on treaties, it could not properly ask the Executive to submit papers having to do with treaties. In the case of Jay's treaty, Hamilton argued, there was the additional consideration that if the treaty were voided, it could well mean war with Great Britain. Finally, if the House could use the appropriation power to sanction or void a treaty, other nations could put no faith in the undertakings of the President, the Secretary of State or American diplomats abroad.

At the same time, Hamilton undertook a campaign to bring

popular pressure on Congress. The line he took in talking and writing to businessmen and other Federalist sympathizers was that support of the treaty meant "the Constitution and Peace," while opposition to it meant "overthrow of the Constitution and War." And he exerted all the influence he could personally on the Congress. He wrote, for example, to his friend William Smith of South Carolina that if the House tried to defeat the treaty, it would "concentre in itself the whole legislative power, and undertake, without the Senate, to repeal a law."

Hamilton's campaign succeeded in stirring up a great deal of activity, and Congress soon received quantities of letters in support of the treaty. Meanwhile, the Federalist senators threatened to refuse to ratify any treaties at all unless the House appropriated the funds for the Jay Treaty. This, of course, was a threat of anarchy from the very guardians of law and order. Hamilton would have no part of such an abuse of power. "Let us be right," he told his friends in the Senate, "because to do right is intrinsically proper." Further, he assured them, "it is the best means of securing final success."

Washington, not waiting for Hamilton's draft of a reply to the House—which was moderate and volunteered to send some of the papers, though not others—flatly refused to send any papers. With both the Executive and the House in an angry mood, the House took up the debate. Ames for the Federalists and Gallatin and Madison for the Republicans played the leading roles. But more significant, no doubt, than speeches was Hamilton's campaign of pressure and intimidation. In the end the vote was 51 to 48 for appropriating the money. The Jay Treaty went into effect. Washington and Hamilton had won another battle; but this time they lost the war. The House passed a resolution asserting its right to inspect any papers relevant to the performance of its duty, and later Presidents have normally thought it politic to consult the House leadership in advance on all major questions of foreign affairs. Anyone who reads a daily paper knows that the Secretary of State and other officials charged with conducting foreign affairs today testify as frequently before House committees as before those of the Senate. In the administration of the nation's fiscal affairs, Alexander Hamilton established a pattern which even his enemies did not seriously disturb when they had the chance. But in the conduct of foreign affairs it was Gallatin and Madison who proved the better—and wiser—prophets.

II

The Presidential election of 1796 came in the tension-filled aftermath of the adoption of Jay's wretched treaty. Things did not look promising for the Federalists. Washington, who had wished to retire as early as 1792, was now adamant. He was going back to Mount Vernon to live out his days well away from the belligerent political atmosphere he hated and feared. Factions, he was persuaded, were the chief cause of social distress. Though he had made repeated efforts to convince Hamilton and Jefferson that they should work in harmony for the good of the country, he had failed because, as James Madison had put it in *Federalist* 10, "the seeds of faction are sown in the nature of man." The point, which Washington never grasped, was not to attempt the impossible task of eliminating factions or parties, but to control them by playing them off against each other, compromising, negotiating, accommodating, but never allowing any one of them, or any combination, to obtain a monopoly of power. Washington, like some later Presidents who affected to be "above politics," appealed to patriotism, asking his colleagues as well as his fellow citizens to suppress their differences in the interests of all. What he did not see was that in a free society the paramount "interest of all" is the freedom to express and to agitate for interests which are not those of all the people but only of some of them.

Hamilton understood this fundamental principle well enough, though he deplored it. The self-interest of man, in fact, was precisely what he undertook to build the nation upon. The point of politics was not to pretend that some other and higher emotion could be brought into play to direct men's actions, but to make it as easy as possible for the interest of the

wealthy and responsible classes to be served. This was a
political goal. For years Washington had been the chief means
of reaching toward it. The best that could be done at the
moment of his retirement was to use his still immense prestige
to denounce parties and factions, in the hope that the public
would be persuaded to accept as his successor a hand-picked
Federalist.

Four years earlier, hoping to retire after one term, Washington had asked Madison to draft for him a suitable "farewell address" to the American people. In 1796 the Madison
draft seemed no longer appropriate. Washington sent it to
Hamilton, asking him to revise or rewrite it as he saw fit.
Hamilton's draft left almost nothing of the original. What was
to become one of the most famous and respected state papers
in the history of the United States became basically a celebra-
tion of the potentials of the American union. On the one
hand, Washington would tell his countrymen, they must keep
aloof from the quarrels of Europe; on the other, they must
subdue the parties and factions at home. It was the latter
point that Hamilton pointed up most vigorously, almost trucu-
lently—and which has been forgotten. But in 1796, when
there was nearly universal agreement on neutralism as a
foreign policy, it was the domestic portions of the address that
were most interesting to Americans. Here are some samples of
the language Hamilton prepared for Washington on this subject:

'Tis allowable to believe that the spirit of party, the
intrigues of foreign nations, the corruption and the ambition of individuals, are likely to prove more formidable
adversaries to the unity of our empire, than any inherent
difficulties in the scheme. 'Tis against these that the
guards of national opinion, national sympathy, national
prudence and virtue are to be erected.

'Tis matter of serious concern that parties in this country
for some time past have been too much characterized by
geographical discriminations . . . which are the mere
artifice of the spirit of party . . .

... the direction of different factions whose passions and prejudices, rather than the true interests of the country, will be too apt to regulate the use of their influence. If it be possible to correct this poison in the affairs of our country, it is worthy the best endeavors of moderate and virtuous men to effect it. . . .

All obstructions to the execution of the laws—all *combinations* and *associations* under whatever plausible character, with the real design to counteract, control, or awe the regular action of the constituted authorities, are contrary to this fundamental principle [the duty of every individual to obey the established government], and of the most fatal tendency. They serve to organize faction, and to put in the stead of the delegated will of the whole nation the will of a party, often a small minority of the whole community; according to the alternate triumph of different parties to make the public administration reflect the schemes and projects of faction rather than the wholesome plans of common councils and deliberations. However combinations or associations of this description may occasionally promote popular ends and purposes, they are likely to produce, in the course of time and things, the most effectual engines by which artful, ambitious, and unprincipled men will be enabled to subvert the power of the people and usurp the reins of government.

... the ordinary and continuous mischiefs of the spirit of party make it the interest and the duty of a wise people to discountenance and repress it.

In the context of their time such passages tell a quite simple story: the President sincerely believed that patriotism could overcome "party spirit"; Alexander Hamilton used the President to identify party spirit and its presumed evils with the Republicans. Thus, while the Federalists tended to form along class lines, the Republicans were more readily identifiable by regional bias—the farmers of the South and West, for example, looked to Jefferson, Madison and Gallatin to shield them from the exploitation of banks and urban business power. The Republicans, again, were the opposition party and therefore to be identified with those "combinations" designed to bring down the government. Finally, Jefferson was popular, more popular than any other American except Washington himself, and so it was necessary to underline the danger that popular measures could be the tricks by which "ambitious and unprincipled men" would seek power.

But to attack the Republicans, even by this inspired device of the beloved and revered Washington's farewell to the people, was not enough. Washington's departure left the Federalists with no obvious leader; in fact, they had no one who could hope to match the popularity of the hated Jefferson. Adams, in Hamilton's view, simply would not do. He was neither a personable nor a popular figure; there was no hope that he could rouse the people to the Federalist cause. And he was egotistical and intractable. In short, he was unlikely to take Hamilton's guidance as Washington had always done. Yet John Adams was the Vice-President, respected by Washington, one of the great patriots of the founding generation, a Federalist at least in his own way, and generally considered to be the heir apparent. How to sidetrack such a man presented a political problem of the first magnitude. Nevertheless Hamilton tackled it—and it turned out to be too much for him.

If Alexander Hamilton had entertained a hope that he might himself become President of the country he had done so much to build, he never said so in public or in private. There was no doubt about his qualifications to conduct the government. He had proved himself a really great administrator, despite opposition criticisms that occasionally found their mark. His ability was universally respected. But his partisanship had been too intense and too personal and the causes he supported too unpopular to make him politically "available." No one knew this better than he. He wasted no time in fruitless efforts on his own behalf. Instead, he decided to try to rally his followers behind a candidate he could quietly manage from the background.

The choice he made was curious, even incomprehensible by modern political criteria. General Thomas Pinckney of South

Carolina was little known outside his native state. For some years he had been serving abroad, as Minister first to Great Britain and then to Spain, where he had negotiated a favorable treaty that partially counterbalanced Jay's. But he was not even well known at the capital. However, Pinckney had fought with great distinction in the Revolution and served afterward as Governor of South Carolina. Four years later, in defending his behavior of 1796, Hamilton even drew a parallel between Pinckney and Washington. If this was gross exaggeration, Pinckney's name, at any rate, was a good one in the South. And this, chiefly, was the point. If the Federalists ran him on the ticket with Adams, Pinckney could be counted on to take some Southern votes away from Jefferson. If the North could be held firmly in the Federalist column, the ticket would win. And if a few Southern electors were to split their votes between Pinckney and Jefferson, leaving Adams out, Pinckney would lead the Federalist ticket. Thus Pinckney would be President and Adams once more Vice-President.

In this stratagem Hamilton's most useful ally was his old friend Congressman William Smith of South Carolina, devout Federalist and bitter critic of Jefferson. While they planned the device of denying the Presidency to Adams, Hamilton and Smith collaborated on a campaign pamphlet against Jefferson—"The Pretensions of Thomas Jefferson to the Presidency Examined." This document, vicious in manner and tone, is a disheartening forecast of a kind of campaign polemic which has often reappeared in American Presidential politics—the theme proposed, usually with some acerbity, that a liberal must be an impractical dreamer, that an intellectual is unfit for office. Among other Presidential candidates, John Quincy Adams, Lincoln, Wilson, Adlai Stevenson and John F. Kennedy were to be victims of this obscurantist tactic.

Jefferson, said Hamilton and Smith, was wholly unfit to be President of the United States. Instead, he should be retired to devote his time to "impaling butterflies and insects, and contriving turnabout chairs for the benefit of his fellow citizens and mankind in general." If, by tragic circumstance, he should become President, his record as a "Deist," "friend of Tom Paine," "cowardly governor of Virginia," etc., guaranteed that he would bring to the country "national disunion, insignificance, disorder, and discredit." If such writing suggests nothing more elevated than the columnists and editors of the radical extremes of the mid-twentieth century, it is fair to say that Hamilton was their lineal ancestor. His immense talents were so often at the disposal of his headstrong personality that in an important sense Hamilton was two different people—an imaginative, skilled and patriotic statesman, and a smart but mean and vulgar political infighter. It can be argued that the tone of political-pamphlet writing in his time was far less disciplined by concern for taste and truth than it was afterward, but it remains an unhappy fact that among the Founding Fathers only Hamilton ever demeaned himself by this kind of writing.

No record exists as to the influence of such pamphlets on the electors. The outcome of the election of 1796, however, suggests that they had little to do with it. Indeed, another and quite different sort of pamphlet may actually have turned the tide against Jefferson just enough to defeat him—a pamphlet which was intended to help him. On orders from his government, French Minister Adet published an "Appeal to the American People," urging the election of Jefferson and rashly threatening the wrath of France if he did not win. This unwonted confirmation of the Federalist line that Jefferson was a creature of the French no doubt hurt him seriously.

As for Hamilton's polemical efforts, they seem to have reached, as on other occasions, only the converted. The Federalists were unanimous in their agreement with Hamilton that Jefferson should be defeated, but they emphatically did not agree that Pinckney should replace Adams as their Presidential candidate. Instead, they split on a sectional basis. New England electors decided to vote solidly for Adams but to give a scattering of votes to various other people instead of equal support to Pinckney. They hoped by this means to make Adams President and Pinckney Vice-President, as a Federalist caucus at Philadelphia in the spring had agreed to do. In his home state Hamilton dared not expose his tactics by asking directly for the dropping of a vote or two from the Adams tally, and New York gave the two men equal votes. In the

South the Pinckney forces were frustrated by the unexpected voting of two Republican electors—one from North Carolina and one from Virginia—who gave their support to Adams instead of Republican Vice-Presidential candidate Aaron Burr. Adams was thus elected by the slight margin of 71 to 68, while Pinckney finished behind Jefferson. For the first and last time in American history an election produced a President of one party and a Vice-President of the other. And with Adams' victory Alexander Hamilton's pretension to national leadership of the Federalist party was rejected. Thereafter he could work effectively for his national purposes only through the agency of others. To be influential he would have to be devious and sometimes unscrupulous. It is testimony to Hamilton's convictions, if not to his character, that he sometimes was both.

III

President Adams, acting, as he hoped, to reassure the nation after the close election, invited all members of Washington's Cabinet to remain in office. They quickly agreed; and because they did so, Adams' administration was doomed to disaster before it ever commenced. These men—Timothy Pickering, Secretary of State; James McHenry, Secretary of War; and Oliver Wolcott, Secretary of the Treasury—were all Hamilton's men, owing their original appointments to his recommendation and devoted not only to his ideas but to him personally. Thus Adams was from the start in the impossible position of trying to run the government with a set of department heads who gave only pro forma recognition to his authority. Happily for government in the United States, no such situation has ever again arisen; all later Presidents have profited by Adams' experience and tried, at least, to make sure that their associates would be loyal to the President. If they have sometimes failed, as did Lincoln, it was because of the personal ambition of Cabinet members, not their loyalty to someone else.

It was through the Cabinet, however, since he could not expect to influence the President, that Alexander Hamilton attempted to run the country from 1797 to 1800, and largely succeeded. McHenry, for example, consulted him on military policy. "My dear Hamilton," he wrote, "will you assist me, or rather your country, with such suggestions and opinions as may occur to you . . . ?" Since Hamilton felt strongly the need for a well trained and equipped standing army and a ready navy, McHenry's invitation provided him with the opportunity to work effectively toward these objectives. The provocative behavior of the French, of course, contributed usefully to his effort.

The first year of John Adams' administration was filled with events as momentous as any the new nation had had to face. France, apparently victorious in her continental wars, decided to menace Great Britain, the only important enemy remaining, by denying her access to European markets and interdicting her supplies wherever possible. This meant interference with American shipping on as large a scale as the size of the French navy would permit. Depredations increased in volume to a point where the United States was forced to act. Would it be war or an effort at peace? Hamilton preferred peace, backed by a strong military establishment. Through McHenry he worked for the building up of military forces. Through Pickering he worked for a diplomatic overture to France.

The French, in retaliation for the recall of American Minister James Monroe by Washington and Pickering in 1796, had refused to receive his successor, General Charles Cotesworth Pinckney. Monroe, of course, was a passionate Jeffersonian Republican who had understandably, if improperly, communicated at length to the French foreign office his resentment of the Jay Treaty after working for two years to soften the blow it was certain to land on French sensibilities. His recall by a Federalist administration was a good deal more sensible than his appointment had been. The French, however, could hardly accept in his place a Federalist friend of Hamilton and the Jay Treaty. Thus the diplomatic situation was anything but promising.

Nevertheless, Hamilton was anxious to give it a try. To refuse to receive a minister who was politically persona non grata, he emphasized to Pickering, was not the same as

[113]

refusing to receive a high commission with plenipotentiary powers to negotiate a settlement that would avoid a war. Such a mission could include an eminent Republican who shared the wish for peace. The best device would be a three-man commission consisting of two Federalists and one Republican. The Republican member, Hamilton suggested, ought to be a man of unquestioned preference for the French "connection," "a leader of the Republican party." This implied, of course, Madison or even Jefferson himself. On such a mission, Hamilton thought, the presence of either of these men would be evidence to the French of American good faith in the desire for peace, while the Republican member could be outvoted by his colleagues if he wished to make too many concessions.

It was an imaginative scheme worthy not only of Hamilton's political insight but of his sincerity in wishing to avoid war. Though he did not know it at the time, his view was emphatically shared by the President. Adams, in fact, asked Madison to undertake the mission. And in a private conversation, he particularly asked Jefferson to intercede in the effort to persuade Madison to accept. The only reason that he did not ask Jefferson himself, he said, was that he did not wish to be criticized by Jefferson's followers for sending him out of the country, where he would be ineffective in domestic politics. It was a generous motive.

Jefferson, for his part, did what he could to persuade Madison to take the appointment. At that time (March, 1797), there was no talk of surrounding him with an unworkable majority of Federalists, as Hamilton was proposing behind the scenes. Madison, however, decided on reflection not to accept. In his old age, Jefferson recorded a conversation with Adams on the subject. When he told the President, on March 6, that Madison had declined, "Adams immediately said, that, on consultation, some objections to the nomination had been raised which he had not contemplated; and was going on with excuses which evidently embarrassed him, when . . . our roads separated and we took leave." Thereafter, Jefferson noted, he was never consulted "as to any measures of the government." No doubt Adams was covering his own hurt pride, but it is likely also that in the interim Hamilton's influence had been felt. At any rate, Adams lost an opportunity for collaboration with Jefferson and Madison which would at the least have greatly altered the history of his administration. Shortly after the election, Jefferson had told Madison that they ought to cooperate with Adams and assure his election to a second term as "perhaps the only sure barrier against Hamilton getting in." Now the moment for such a possible alliance was gone, and the way was left clear for Hamilton, not to the Presidency itself, which was never a real possibility, but to dominate the administration of John Adams.

However, his audacious plan for a bipartisan mission to France was not well received by many of his Federalist friends. Why appease the deadly enemy of the very system of government they were trying to safeguard? If a mission must be sent, let it at least be composed of reliable men who would make no concessions. With Jefferson and Madison out of the picture, the President agreed to the latter plan. To the mission he named C. C. Pinckney, John Marshall and his old friend from Massachusetts Elbridge Gerry. Forthwith Gerry and Marshall sailed for France to join Pinckney and to pass presently into history as the protagonists of the notorious XYZ affair.

IV

While the American people waited for word from the mission in Paris, Alexander Hamilton's political and personal fortunes took a wholly unexpected and probably fatal jolt. The clerk of the House of Representatives at that time was one John Beckley, a long-time Republican and energetic propagandist. Beckley was a friend of Jefferson's and a member of the "in group" around Madison and Gallatin at Philadelphia. In early 1797, the Federalist caucus in the House, encouraged by the election of 1796, understandably decided to oust him. They succeeded in mustering a majority and Beckley was removed. It turned out to be a costly act, for Beckley was well prepared to get revenge. In his possession were all the papers connected with the presumably forgotten Hamilton-Reynolds affair of years before. His secretary had transcribed the documents collected by Muhlenberg, Monroe and Venable, and Beckley had carefully preserved copies of them. These he now turned over to publicist James Callender, one of the meanest scoundrels then at large. In later years this so-called Republican was to break the scandal that forced President Jefferson's public admission of improper conduct in his youth. But now, in 1797, he proceeded to blacken the reputation of Alexander Hamilton.

Callender's serial pamphlet, *The History of the United States for the Year 1796,* was the vehicle for the Beckley-Callender revelations. Hamilton was charged with conspiracy to invest public funds in illegal personal speculation. Reynolds, with suggestive quotations from the correspondence, was represented as one of Hamilton's partners, but only one. Callender suggested that there may well have been as many as twenty others. As for the clearing of Hamilton's honor by the three members of Congress in 1792, Callender dismissed it by simply pointing out that congressmen could be expected to lie for each other!

It was a desperate situation for Hamilton—but not, he hoped, irretrievable. He could go to Muhlenberg, Venable and Monroe and ask their intercession. They were in honor bound to state publicly their belief in Hamilton's innocence. Muhlenberg and Venable responded to his appeal immediately, as Hamilton assumed they would. But James Monroe did not, and a sordid chapter of American history ensued.

When Monroe failed to answer, Hamilton wrote to him again. Again there was no reply. At this point Hamilton learned that Monroe was in New York and called upon him personally. To understand this crucial interview and the correspondence that followed, it is necessary to know not only the state of Hamilton's mind—which was, of course, highly agitated—but also that of Monroe's. The Virginian had recently returned from Paris, where he had certainly been very badly used by the Federalist administration. The story of his mission is not a part of the life of Alexander Hamilton and details would not be appropriate here. But Hamilton had joined in the plan to send a prominent Republican to Paris to try to counteract the effect of Jay's mission to London; Monroe knew, in 1797, that Hamilton had drafted Jay's instructions, which he, Monroe, had never been allowed to see; Monroe had not only been recalled "in disgrace," as President Adams had publicly stated, but Secretary of State Pickering, Hamilton's friend, had even refused to honor Monroe's expense accounts. Monroe, for the moment, had become the focal point of Republican opposition to the administration. He was writing a pamphlet to vindicate his own conduct and reveal the duplicity of Federalist policy toward France. Alexander Hamilton he considered the evil genius of the Federalist party, which, in turn, he believed to be dedicated to the destruction of republican democracy—and all leading Republicans—and the restoration of monarchy.

In short, James Monroe was in no mood to help Alexander Hamilton rescue *his* reputation. Indeed, he had never been quite sure that he and his colleagues had been right in accepting Hamilton's story. Hamilton, as he cast his mind back to the scene in Philadelphia in 1792, seemed to remember that Monroe had said little and had accepted the Reynolds story with evident lack of enthusiasm. But he had accepted it. And as the two men met in New York in 1797, Hamilton called upon Monroe directly to honor that old commitment. Monroe, for his part, let Hamilton know exactly how he felt about him. It was a tense moment. Monroe finally resolved it, or so Hamilton believed, by agreeing to see Muhlenberg and Venable in Philadelphia and draw up with them a suitable paper to exculpate Hamilton of the charge of misconduct in office.

In a letter to Hamilton dated July 17, 1797, Monroe and Muhlenberg did in fact reiterate their satisfaction with Hamilton's explanation of the Reynolds affair as given in 1792. They also disclaimed any responsibility for the publication of Callender's documents.

But among these documents was a memorandum, made and signed by Monroe, *after* Hamilton's explanation of 1792 had been accepted, in which he recorded a charge by Jacob Clingman that Hamilton's explanation was a cover story and that letters he had submitted to prove it were forgeries. Clingman then reiterated his claim that Hamilton was guilty of speculating with public funds. Now, in July of 1797, the whole wretched controversy turned upon this document. Only Monroe's name appeared on it, thus only Monroe could testify that he placed no credence in it. Hamilton, therefore, after properly acknowledging the letter from Muhlenberg and Monroe, wrote separately to Monroe for "some explanation of the note of January 2, 1793, with your signature only," since it might be "inferred . . . that you meant to give credit and sanction to the suggestion that the defence set by me was an imposition."

Monroe's reply was the first of a series in which he seemed, at least to Hamilton, to equivocate to such an extent as to confirm the suspicion that he gave some credence to Clingman's claims. "I neither meant to give nor imply any opinion of my own as to its contents," Monroe wrote Hamilton. Obviously this was not satisfactory. It would, Hamilton told Monroe, be open to "inference, that the information of Clingman had revived the suspicions which my explanation had removed. . . . I therefore request you to say whether this inference be intended." Monroe simply reiterated his statement that he "did not mean to convey any opinion" of his own.

Hamilton was not only disturbed at the possibilities that might arise from Monroe's conduct, he was furious at Monroe's continued equivocation. He now told Monroe that to "have given or intended to give the least sanction or credit, after all that was known to you, to the mere assertion of either of three persons—Clingman, Reynolds, or his wife— would have betrayed a disposition toward me which, if it appeared to exist, would merit epithets the severest that I could apply." This was strong language, despite the "ifs." This time Monroe replied at some length. He pointed out to Hamilton that "we did not bind ourselves," as was fair enough, "not to hear further information on the subject, or even not to proceed further in case we found it our duty so to do." Monroe reminded Hamilton that he had never seen fit to proceed, but that now the documents were made public, he still reserved his opinion of Clingman's statement until he had heard Hamilton's "defense."

That Monroe was now implying a question about Hamilton's integrity could scarcely be doubted. The only proper reply, as Hamilton saw it, was to impugn Monroe's motives and to do so through a second—thus indicating his willingness to settle the matter in a duel. "The result to my mind," he wrote, summing up his interpretation of Monroe's various letters, "is that you have been and are actuated by motives towards me malignant and dishonorable." Monroe replied, again at length, disclaiming any wish to duel but stating his willingness to accept a challenge. At the same time he repeated his fixed position that his signature on the record of the Clingman statement "never intended to convey an opinion upon it." Hamilton now told Monroe the subject was "too disgusting to leave me any inclination to prolong the discussion of it." He had been driven, he said, to give a public explanation that "must decide, as far as public opinion is concerned, between us." The appeal, he admitted, would be "painful," but "in the principal point it must completely answer my purpose."

Hamilton had, in fact, for several days been drafting an article which would lay the whole matter, documents and all, before the public. Faced with the problem of defending his honor as a public servant by revealing his unfaithfulness, or remaining silent to let the libels continue unchecked, he had decided to tell the truth. It no longer mattered what Monroe did or said.

Nevertheless, the two men came very close to a duel. Hamilton's second delivered what was almost a challenge. Monroe named Aaron Burr to act for him, thus underlining the political significance of the issue. Burr wisely undertook to resolve the matter without a duel, and succeeded by the simple device of not delivering Monroe's final communication. And so Alexander Hamilton lived to fight a fatal duel with Burr himself, while James Monroe lived on much longer to become, as fifth President of the United States, the solemn symbol of the very nationalism Alexander Hamilton had fostered with such flamboyant devotion. Needless to say, when Hamilton's public confession appeared, Betsy stood loyally by him. And the storm at last passed over.

V

When John Marshall and Charles Cotesworth Pinckney reported from France that their overtures had been met not by diplomatic negotiation but by the demand for a personal bribe to Talleyrand and a "loan" to the government of France that amounted to blackmail, John Adams was almost overcome by righteous fury. The fact that Gerry remained in Paris after the others left, apparently under threat from Talleyrand that France would declare war if he departed, was simply unacceptable to a sovereign nation. Adams saw at that stage no alternative to war. He instructed the small United States Navy to give what protection it could to American merchant vessels and ordered defiance of French decrees against American commerce. Thus began the undeclared war that precipitated the ruin of the Adams administration. Gerry, it should be added, disagreed with his colleagues, opposed Adams' new policy, and upon his return, in a famous letter to Jefferson, became a Republican and eventually Vice-President under Madison.

It is hard to find fault with Adams' belligerence under the circumstances of 1797. Nevertheless, Alexander Hamilton, so long the avowed enemy of the French Revolution and the devoted supporter of an "English connection," displayed the statesmanship of which he was always capable by defending as long as he could the unpopular cause of peace. "I wish," he said, "to see a temperate, but grave, solemn, and firm communication from the President." Meanwhile, he urged full-scale preparation of the nation's defenses. The best American policy, he said, was "to meet the aggressions upon us by proportionate resistance, and to prepare vigorously for further resistance."

However, when it became apparent that the French would not change their policy, Hamilton was for war—defensive war, but war nevertheless. In private correspondence he made his views clear to Pickering and McHenry; and he went again to the newspapers to rally his countrymen. Once more he denounced the Republicans as "the unfaithful and guilty leaders of a foreign faction." Honest men of all parties, he wrote, "will unite to maintain and defend the honor and the sovereignty of their country. The crisis demands it. 'Tis folly to dissemble. The despots of France are waging war against us." The problem now, he said, "is whether we will maintain or surrender our sovereignty. To maintain it with firmness is the most sacred of duties, the most glorious of tasks."

Under the circumstances, Hamilton might have been expected to place himself at the disposal of the President. And so he did, but not by direct communication. He well knew he could expect nothing from Adams. Even the members of the Cabinet might not have enough influence to obtain for Hamilton the post he thought he ought to have in the oncoming war—inspector general of the armies. Once more, and for the last time, his appeal was to the venerable Washington. By combining the influence of Washington with the advice of the Cabinet, Hamilton might yet come close to commanding the army.

For there was no doubt that Washington himself would have to come out of retirement to become once again Commander in Chief. That title by the Constitution belonged to Adams, but no one, least of all Adams himself, supposed that so unmilitary a President could lead the troops in the field.

In May, 1798, Hamilton began to work on Washington. At first he resorted to a kind of sincere flattery he well knew the old General would find acceptable. "At the present dangerous crisis of public affairs," he wrote, "I make no apology for troubling you with a political letter." While sentiment for a strong posture against France was prevalent in the North and East, Hamilton was much concerned about the South. Here was where Washington could help: "I have asked myself," he told the General, "whether it might not be expedient for you to make a circuit through Virginia and North Carolina, under some pretence of health, etc. This would call forth addresses, public dinners, etc., which would give you an opportunity of expressing sentiments in answers, toasts, etc., which would throw the weight of your character into the scale of the government and revive an enthusiasm for your person, that may be turned into the right channel." Washington presently rejected this suggestion, as Hamilton no doubt was sure he would. "The suggestion," he said, "was an indigested thought, begotten by my anxiety."

But the exchange had opened the way for Hamilton to take up with his old chief the matter of where and how he should serve in the army that was to be rebuilt. "You intimate a desire to be informed what would be my part in such an event as to entering the military service. I have no scruple," he confessed, "about opening myself to you on this point." The point was that if he was to go into the army, he would have to be invited "to a station in which the service I may render may be proportionate to the sacrifice I am to make." The post he wanted, he said quite frankly, was inspector general, under Washington, "with a command in the line." He went on to say that he had "no knowledge of any arrangement contemplated," which was not candid, since he was well aware from McHenry that Adams was thinking of inviting Revolutionary officers to return to active duty at the last rank they had held. Since men like Knox and C. C. Pinckney, as well as a good many others who might be called up, had been general officers, Colonel Hamilton's prospects on this principle were not promising. By letting Washington know what he wanted, he was setting events in train to undo the President's plan. After some months he succeeded.

Meanwhile, he was writing to Wolcott and McHenry with detailed advice about building up the military establishment. Among other things he proposed to establish "an academy for naval and military instruction." It was not until 1802, when Thomas Jefferson was President and Hamilton's influence in public affairs permanently ended, that the United States Military Academy at West Point was founded. But Hamilton's suggestion gave impetus to the movement for professional training of American officers, just as the small fleet of fast boats he had organized in earlier years to prevent smuggling was to become the United States Coast Guard.

While Hamilton was maneuvering for a satisfactory appointment in the army and working to give that army adequate manpower and supplies, the Federalist-dominated Congress was reacting to the undeclared war with France by passing laws that would suppress any serious opposition to the government. For the first but, unhappily, not the last time, some Americans were prepared to protect the nation by suppressing the very liberties that other Americans thought made the nation worth preserving. "When a man is heard to inveigh against the Sedition Law," said the Federalist *New York Commercial Advertiser,* "set him down as one who would submit to no restraint which is calculated for the peace of society. He deserves to be suspected."

But Alexander Hamilton, a genuine conservative, could not approve such measures. "If an alien bill passes," he told Pickering, "I would like to know what policy, in execution, is likely to govern the Executive." His own opinion was that while "the mass ought to be obliged to leave the country . . . there ought to be guarded exceptions of characters whose situation would expose them too much if sent away." Since "the mass" was a meaningless term and the only people likely to be "sent away" were men like DuPont, Priestley and Volney, precisely those "whose situation would expose them too much," Hamilton was saying that he hoped the Executive would nullify the law in administering it.

When he saw the draft of the sedition bill a few days later, Hamilton was even more disturbed. He wrote hastily to Wolcott to urge caution. The letter is worth quoting in full:

Dear Sir:

I have this moment seen a bill brought into the Senate entitled "A Bill to define more particularly the crime of treason," etc. There are provisions in this bill, which, according to a cursory view, appear to me highly exceptionable, and such as, more than anything else, may engender civil war. I have not time to point out my objections by this post, but I will do it tomorrow. I hope sincerely the thing may not be hurried through. Let us not establish a tyranny. Energy is a very different thing from violence. If we make no false step, we shall be essentially united, but if we push things to an extreme, we shall then give to faction body and solidity.

This sound and patriotic advice was, of course, not heeded. The Alien and Sedition bills became law and, as Hamilton had foretold, all but precipitated a civil war. Only his long-standing distrust of Jefferson and Madison enabled him to square with his conscience the political necessity of defending the laws against the Kentucky and Virginia Resolutions.

Through the remaining months of the year, Hamilton continued his efforts to bypass his military seniors, Knox, Pinckney and others, by appeals to McHenry, Pickering and, of course, Washington. He couched all his letters in terms flattering to the other men but firmly emphasizing his own greater service since the Revolution and unashamedly asserting his superior ability. Adams resisted pettishly, and understandably, until in October Washington made a direct request for Hamilton's appointment. Adams yielded, and at the age of forty-three Alexander Hamilton achieved his lifetime ambition to become a ranking general. With Washington at the top of the command, he had little reason to doubt that his own influence in military affairs would thereafter be decisive.

And it was. One of the first tasks he faced, together with Washington and Pinckney, was the commissioning of officers in the new army. An important candidate for a brigadier general's baton was Aaron Burr. Hamilton favored the appointment, and if it had been granted, the two men might finally have worked together instead of fatally apart. Hamilton wrote Wolcott that he "had some reasons for wishing that the administration may manifest a cordiality to him." Burr might prove "a useful cooperator," and though others did not agree, Hamilton thought "the case is worth the experiment." But the haughty Burr wrecked his chances by his manner at a hearing before Hamilton and Pinckney. When asked whether he would loyally support Washington as Commander in Chief, he said frankly that though of course he would be loyal, "he despised Washington as a man of no talents, and one who could not spell a sentence of common English." After his application was understandably rejected, Burr reported the matter to the President. "I reproved Burr," Adams noted, "for this sally and said his prejudice made him very unreasonable, for to my certain knowledge Washington was not so illiterate." What he thought of Washington's talents, however, seems clear enough!

As the war effort developed, Hamilton acted more and more like a combination of Commander in Chief and Secretary of War. His letters to McHenry were often peremptory, more like orders than requests. If McHenry showed the slightest resistance to a Hamilton proposal, which he rarely did, the inspector general would employ the faithful Wolcott to get the business done. For example, Hamilton wrote to Wolcott on April 8, 1799: "I sent you in confidence the copy of a letter of this date to the Secretary of War and of the plan to which it refers. Consider it well. Make the Secretary of War talk about it, without letting him know that I have sent it to you. The proper course in the interest of the army is indicated by the plan I present."

The President kept out of military matters, or was kept out of them, almost entirely. He understood well enough how he had lost his authority, but without directly attacking Washington, he could do little about it. Hamilton was well shielded, and also efficient. Adams' state of mind, under the circumstances, is revealed by his caustic comment that all the forts built under Hamilton's direction were named after Hamilton himself, or McHenry, or even Pickering, but "not one of them had been called *Adams,* except perhaps a diminutive work at Rhode Island."

With the President in the background perforce, Alexander Hamilton became increasingly bold. At times he effectively assumed Presidential authority for himself. Thus, in response to a request from Federalist Congressman Harrison Gray Otis, he advocated a standby declaration of war:

I should be glad to see, before the close of the session, a law empowering the President, at his discretion, in case a negotiation between the United States and France should not be on foot by the first of August next, or being on foot should terminate without an adjustment of differences, to declare that a state of war exists between the two countries.

[125]

Again, in correspondence with Rufus King, Minister to London, he suggested that King propose an alliance with Great Britain to "liberate" the Latin American colonies of Spain. And in February, 1799, he gave directions to Theodore Sedgwick, a Federalist leader in the House, as to what should be done about the Kentucky and Virginia Resolutions against the Alien and Sedition laws: a special committee of Congress should publish a report condemning the two legislatures, placing blame not on the people but on Republican leaders, "measures for raising the military force should proceed with activity," and "let them be drawn toward Virginia, for which there is an obvious pretext." In all such matters of the greatest concern to the government and the nation, Hamilton acted without consulting the President, indeed entirely ignoring him. It was fortunate for the country that before any of these ideas were acted upon, Adams stunned Hamilton and the Federalists by deciding to become President himself in fact as well as in name.

On February 18, 1799, without consulting anybody, least of all the Cabinet agents of Alexander Hamilton, John Adams sent to the Senate the nomination of William Vans Murray to be Minister to France. The President had received from various sources what he considered to be peace feelers from the French government. At his farm in Braintree he had thought long and prayerfully over what was the best course. His decision was to try for peace. Under the shock of this startling reversal of policy, the Congress did not know what to do. Hamilton thought Adams had lost his mind; "passion," he said, "wrests the helm from reason."

But Adams was sincere, rational and insistent. Despite the efforts of Hamilton and others, the Congress, with massive Republican support, authorized the mission to France and the Senate approved it, only adding Oliver Ellsworth and Patrick Henry to make it a three-man commission. However, the continuing pressure of Pickering and Hamilton succeeded in delaying the departure of these envoys for many months.

When the President went up to Braintree in the spring, the Hamiltonians considered a plan to seize the government from his hands in something like a *coup d'état.* "If there was everywhere, a disposition, without prejudice and nonsense," Hamilton wrote McHenry, "to concert a rational plan, I would cheerfully come to Philadelphia and assist in it; nor can I doubt that success may be insured." If he had never been an advocate of monarchy, Hamilton was now at any rate prepared to be a dictator.

How could the Federalist leadership have reached a point of such desperation because of the President's decision to try for peace? How could so sophisticated a man as Alexander Hamilton have so lost his political bearings? One answer is to be found in the nature of the issues. Just as the Jeffersonian Republicans were determined, at any cost, to reverse the course of American policy and democratize the country, so the "high" Federalists, the Hamiltonians, were resolved that this should not happen. Adams' desire to make peace placed him, in their view, in the camp of the Republican "Jacobins," the friends of France who were bent on ruining the new nation. These convictions were not rhetorical only; they were matters quite literally of personal honor, even of life and death. As early as 1796, Republican John Taylor and Federalist Rufus King had been corresponding on possible terms for breaking up the Union. The "discipline of democracy," the essential willingness to abide by the will of the majority by which a free republic must conduct its business, had not yet become the first priority of the public men of the United States or of their followers. To make peace with France seemed to the Hamiltonians the ultimate sell-out. It was intolerable.

Another explanation lies in the purposes and ambition of Alexander Hamilton himself. If peace should come about, his developing plans to lead the army against French possessions in the western hemisphere, to drive out the Spanish from the West and from Mexico, would have to be abandoned. Hamilton well knew the American people would never support wars of outright conquest. An empire—with himself at its head—could be won as a by-product of a patriotic war against France; there was no other means. In the state of mind to which his long frustrated ambitions had brought him by 1799,

Hamilton was quite literally prepared to go to any length to keep the war going.

He even made a personal appeal to Adams. Leaving his troops without permission, he called on the President at Trenton, New Jersey, and pleaded with him not to allow the peace mission to sail. His argument was that the allied powers, under the leadership of Great Britain, were about to win the European war. If the United States should make peace with France now, the British would surely declare war on the United States as soon as France had fallen, if not sooner. He claimed to have reliable information from Europe to support his position. Adams, who received him courteously, noted that he had never in his life heard "a man talk more like a fool." It was of course a hopeless mission that Hamilton had undertaken. His own dogmatic certainty about foreign affairs was more than matched by Adams', and the President could add the clinching observation that he himself was a veteran of European diplomacy while Hamilton had never been out of the country.

After that episode, Hamilton made one more somewhat feeble if strikingly improper effort. He wrote Ellsworth, urging him not to go to France. But the Chief Justice, though he agreed to counsel delay, would not deliberately counter the wishes of the President. The envoys sailed, with advance word that they would be well received.

There was little for the army Hamilton was building to do. No doubt prolonged and frustrating inactivity accounts in part for the great show of force to put down the "insurrection" of 1799. On this occasion, when a handful of Pennsylvania farmers led by one Fries stormed a jail where some other farmers had been lodged for refusing to pay taxes, the President dispatched several thousand troops under a brigadier general. This accorded with Hamilton's advice to McHenry. "Beware, my dear sir," he told the Secretary of War, "of magnifying a riot into an insurrection by employing in the first instance an inadequate force." The actual resistance had already long subsided by the time the army arrived. Northampton County was nevertheless invested for months lest the "Fries' Rebellion" kindle a "Jacobin Revolution." For once Adams and Hamilton were in agreement.

It is interesting to observe that Adams regained his composure much sooner than did Hamilton. In the spring of 1800, while the Justice Department was trying to convict Fries of treason under the Sedition law, the President suddenly decided that the whole affair was silly. Against the advice of Hamilton and the Cabinet, he pardoned Fries and all the others involved. "What good, what example would have been exhibited to the nation," Adams wanted to know, "by the execution of three or four obscure, miserable Germans, as ignorant of our language as they were of our laws, and the nature and definition of treason?" It was fair testimony to the irresponsibility of both parties that while the Federalists wished to execute men for what at worst was only a misdemeanor under the law—"an example," said Hamilton, was "indispensable to . . . security"—the Republicans were guilty of stirring up the whole matter in the first place by spreading false and malicious rumors that Adams was going to mortgage all the real property in the country and marry his son to a daughter of George III!

VI

In the spring of 1800, two matters above all others claimed the attention of the American people and of General Hamilton. The first was the trickle of news coming from Europe and suggesting that the negotiations in Paris were proceeding favorably. At the same time, French depredations on American shipping were halted, giving substance to the tenuous reports. The second matter was the approaching Presidential election, in which Adams was to be challenged once more by Thomas Jefferson.

By this time Hamilton had already fought the first electoral battle of the campaign—and lost it. The New York elections of 1799 had determined which Presidential candidate would get that state's electoral vote, since the votes for elector were cast at that time by state legislatures. Hamilton had exerted every bit of influence he could command to help the Federalists hold control of the legislature, but the unpopularity of the war with France, opposition to the Alien and Sedition laws, and a general mood of resentment against the Federalists brought a Republican victory. In the contest the Republicans of New York City were led by Aaron Burr. Thus the political issue was directly joined. Burr won because he had the better issues and because, as he himself said, he had better "management." Burr, in short, had in Tammany Hall what was to become proverbial in American politics—a "well-oiled political machine." Hamilton had money and some devoted lieutenants; but his political army lacked privates.

Knowing full well the significance of Burr's victory, he was not inclined merely to accept it. The device he hit upon to frustrate the will of the New York voters was hardly defensible on any standard of political fair play. To Governor John Jay he proposed that the legislature—the lame duck legislature—be called into special session to write a new law covering the choice of Presidential electors. The idea was to have them chosen by the voters according to election districts instead of by the legislature. Under such a system, at least a substantial minority of Federalist electors would, of course, be chosen, while if the Republican-dominated legislature appointed them, all the electors would be Republican.

The plan had the specious appearance of being democratic. But since it was to be enacted by the repudiated legislature for the purpose of obviating the objective for which the new legislature had been elected, it was hardly less than dishonest. At least Hamilton was clearheaded about it. "In times like these," he told Jay, "it will not do to be over-scrupulous." The objective of preventing Jefferson from becoming President was great enough to warrant almost any measure. "It is easy to sacrifice the substantial interests of society by a strict adherence to ordinary rules," he argued. The "substantial interest" was "to prevent an atheist in religion, and a fanatic in politics from getting possession of the helm of state." Fortunately, Jay would not demean himself to act on such a stratagem. He sent no reply to Hamilton at all, only noting for his file that it was "a measure for party purposes it would not become me to adopt."

And so Hamilton had to go into the Presidential election campaign of 1800 without the electors of his own state to stand back of his leadership. It proved an insuperable handicap. He nevertheless made one more bold effort to unseat Adams. The plan he recommended to his political friends around the country was similar to the one that had failed in 1796, namely, to withhold some Federalist votes from Adams while giving them to the Vice-Presidential candidate. The second man on the Adams ticket in 1800 was Charles Cotesworth Pinckney, a North Carolinian no more and no less estimable than his brother Thomas. The difference between them was that Charles Cotesworth was a willing participant in the Hamiltonian scheme, while Thomas had not been party to the doings of 1796 in his behalf.

The continuing good news from France led to the gradual demobilization of the army and, in the spring of 1800, General Hamilton made a tour of New England to bid farewell to his troops. Wherever he went he was well received, and the speeches he made were so full of charm and patriotism that his tour was a rather startling series of triumphs, in view at least of the political misfortunes that had befallen him or that he had brought upon himself. But the fond farewells to the soldiers were only a small part of his purpose in New England. He was using the tour openly and frankly, to campaign against Adams, and to urge the election of Pinckney. The President, he told the Federalist leaders, was "a very unfit and incapable character, excessively vain and jealous and ignobly attached to place."

When Adams learned of Hamilton's campaign, he was nearly apoplectic. Hamilton, he announced, was a "bastard," and the leader of a "damned faction of British partisans." By comparison he greatly preferred Jefferson. "Mr. Jefferson is an infinitely better man . . . a wiser one I am sure; and if President, will act wisely. I know it, and would sooner be Vice President under him, or even Minister Resident at the Hague, than to be indebted to such a being as Hamilton for the Presidency." This time, as it turned out, Adams and Hamilton were in agreement—they each preferred Jefferson to the other! "If we must have an enemy at the head of the government," said Hamilton, "let it be one whom we can óppose, and for whom we are not responsible."

In May, convinced finally that he had been all along duped and cheated by Hamilton, Adams fired Pickering and McHenry. Pickering refused to resign and was simply given notice of dismissal. Wolcott, for some curious and still obscure reason, continued to hold the President's confidence. Adams certainly knew that Wolcott had been Hamilton's man from the early days under Washington; yet he kept him on in the Treasury, where he could and did keep up the flow of intelligence to his real chief in New York.

Hamilton's final shot in the campaign was a long pamphlet directed against the President personally. He was repeatedly and emphatically advised against the idea; only Pickering, embittered by his dismissal, encouraged him. But Hamilton needed no encouragement. That he seriously thought his attack would defeat Adams and elect Pinckney seems doubtful. He must have realized that the more likely outcome would be the defeat of the Federalist ticket, and it seems reasonable to suppose that by the summer of 1800 he was prepared to contemplate that result. Rarely if ever in American history has one leading national figure been so publicly unrestrained in his hatred of another. Hamilton had never had a taste for politics and only occasionally displayed any skill in it. Now he abandoned politics altogether in favor of character assassination. He even stooped to asking Pickering to carry away with him, when he left office, copies of papers "such as will enable you to explain both Jefferson and Adams. You are aware," he said, "of a very curious journal of the latter when he was in Europe—a tissue of weakness and vanity." Pickering did not scruple to comply with this request.

On August 1, Hamilton wrote Adams an insolent letter (he told Pickering it was "polite") intended to force him to repudiate his rumored denunciation of Hamilton as head of a "British faction." "I must, sir," he wrote, "take it for granted that you cannot have made such assertions or insinuations without being willing to avow them, and to assign the reasons to a party who may conceive himself injured by them." But Adams was too sophisticated, despite his rages, to be trapped.

He never replied and Hamilton had to content himself two months later with a still more insolent note. "From this silence I will draw no inference," he said, "nor will I presume to judge of the fitness of silence on such an occasion on the part of the chief magistrate of a republic towards a citizen who, without stain, has discharged so many important public trusts." That the writer of this pompous note should have been concerned about the vanity of John Adams is both an unhappy irony and a revelation of the state of Hamilton's mind.

The pamphlet itself did not appear until too late to be useful as a campaign document, but not too late to bring down public opprobrium upon its author. It was written with a good deal of Hamilton's old-time sharpness and wit. But it was so obviously self-serving and so meanly invidious that it became rather a scandal in itself than an effective attack on the President.

In view of Hamilton's behavior after the election, the miserable attack on Adams appears almost as though it had served its author as a purgative. For when his party touched the bottom of intended corruption and subversion of the republic, Alexander Hamilton acted decisively with the patriotic statesmanship that had always been a major element in his sadly complex character.

VII

The story of the election of 1800 has often been told. The Republican ticket won by 73 votes to Adams' 65. Pinckney received 64. The votes for Burr and Jefferson were by accident evenly divided. It had been intended that one or two Burr votes should be held out to make sure that Jefferson was President and Burr Vice-President. But either Burr himself had failed to play his part in New York or someone else in some other state had slipped. At any rate, there was a tie to be resolved. And here the Federalists saw a desperate chance to salvage something from the lost election.

The plan, to which some of Hamilton's close friends were a party, was to employ Federalist votes in the House of Representatives to break the tie that would result if the Republicans did not first make sure that Jefferson had more votes than Burr, and they would break it in favor of Burr. In order to make sure of success, it was necessary to secure Burr's cooperation. Various overtures were made to him suggesting that if he would agree to preserve Federalist policy, he could have the Presidency. Burr, of course, knew that this was contrary to the will of the people and would make a mockery of the election. Much as he wished the highest office, he had not quite sufficient temerity to make the deal. But he did nothing to prevent the Federalists from acting on his behalf. To Jefferson and other Republicans he expressed his loyalty and entire willingness to serve under Jefferson. He even indicated to Jefferson that he would withdraw and serve in the Cabinet if that was Jefferson's preference. He assured his party that the New York electors would do their duty. But he made no move to have votes for himself withheld.

The Federalist proposal was nothing less than a conspiracy to give the Presidency to a man who had been elected to the Vice-Presidency. Alexander Hamilton would have no part in it, and as soon as he learned of it, did his best to forestall it. This time his best was sufficient. As early as December 16, he was urging Wolcott to use his influence in New England to discourage such action. "Jefferson is to be preferred," he said; "he is by far not so dangerous a man; and he has pretensions to character." This was uncommon generosity to come from Hamilton's usually vitriolic pen. But he was not prepared to see constitutional processes flaunted even to defeat his ancient enemy. Both policy and honor were at stake. He knew Burr, as he wrote in long and repetitious letters to Sedgwick, Gouverneur Morris, James A. Bayard and others, and Burr was a man of no principles at all, only ambition to rule. "His ambition will not be content," he wrote, "with those objects which virtuous men of either party will allot to it, and his situation and his habits will oblige him to have recourse to corrupt expedients, from which he will be restrained by no moral scruple." And again, "Adieu to the Federal Troy, if they once introduce this Grecian horse into their citadel."

At the same time, the proposed convention with France had been laid before the Senate, and Federalist senators favored rejecting it. Hamilton linked the convention and the election in his pleas to his friends. To reject the convention would be almost as dishonorable as to give the Presidency to Burr. In practical terms it was not a bad agreement, and "the leaving of the whole subject open will render it easy for the Jacobin administration to make a worse thing." To ratify the convention would not unduly annoy the British and would be politically expedient for the Federalist party. "The contrary would finish the ruin of the federal party," he told Morris, "and endanger our internal tranquillity." In sum, "the convention with France ought to be ratified as the least of two evils" and "on the same ground Jefferson ought to be preferred to Burr." "If there be a man in the world I ought to hate, it is Jefferson," he said (for the moment forgetting John Adams!). "With Burr I have always been personally well. But the public good must be paramount to every private consideration." Ultimately, Alexander Hamilton would stand on principle and honor, no matter how bitter the medicine he had to take.

What apparently decided the issue was a long letter he wrote to Bayard, Delaware congressman, on January 16. Bayard was under very great pressure because, as the sole congressman from his state, he personally would determine its vote for President in case of a tie in the electoral college being referred to the House. He had indicated to Hamilton that he was wavering. He had, he said, resolved to "hold himself disengaged" till the moment of final decision. In his letter Hamilton recapitulated all the arguments he had been urging—Burr's character, Jefferson's caution, etc. But the overpowering argument was that both parties would lose by Burr's election. As President, Hamilton said, "he will never choose to lean on good men, because he knows that they will never support his bad projects; but instead of this he will endeavor to disorganize both parties, and to form out of them a third, composed of men fitted by their characters to be conspirators and instruments of such projects." Finally, and he must have gritted his teeth to write it, "very very confidential —In my opinion he is inferior in real ability to Mr. Jefferson." A few days later he sent an urgent note to Sedgwick, calling attention to this letter to Bayard and once more telling his friends that the Federalists would "rue the preference" if they gave it to the modern "Catiline."

Bayard did not, despite the pressure from Hamilton, actually make up his mind until "the ultimate moment of decision." It was the thirty-sixth ballot on February 17 before he acted to break the deadlock. When he did so, Thomas Jefferson was elected, as the people had intended. But he owed his election in the end more to Alexander Hamilton than to any other man. Thus in the moment of his final defeat on the national stage, Hamilton shared in the triumph of Jefferson. If it was not poetic justice, it was certainly high drama. Before the denouement there was still to be one more magnificent moment.

Chapter 6

THE BITTER END

I

Thomas Jefferson had been President of the United States only a few months when, in a private letter, he paid an unintentional compliment to Alexander Hamilton which would have reassured that out-of-office statesman had he known of it. It might, in some degree perhaps, have vindicated his choice of Jefferson over Burr. "When this government was established," said the President, "it was possible to have kept it going on true principles but the contracted, English, half-lettered ideas of Hamilton destroyed that hope in the bud. We can pay off his debts in fifteen years: but we can never get rid of his financial system." Without doing too much violence to them, Hamilton might have translated these words into something quite different: "When this government was established it was possible that it would flounder in the same anarchy and incompetence that had plagued its predecessor. But my efforts to build stable fiscal and financial institutions and a workable system of federal public administration over the rebellious states, borrowing from British experience where it was relevant, were in some measure successful. Now, twelve years later, the undisciplined democrats, having come to power on the springboard of demagoguery, can retire the public debt—and suffer serious economic consequences—but they cannot destroy the institutions I have built. In the long run the nation will be secure." Both men, of course, were right—and wrong—as they had been all along. But it was now Jefferson's turn, not so much to upset the Hamiltonian system as to provide for it a broader basis of public control.

The creator of the federal structure, now finally retired from the national government, returned to his law practice in New York. He felt defeated and discouraged. "What can I do better than withdraw from the scene?" he asked Morris. "Every day proves to me more and more that this American world was not made for me." The four short years that were left to him were to be years of heartbreak, with moments of triumph, then final disaster.

II

Hamilton's retirement began with an important achievement. With the Jeffersonians triumphant and the Federalists "disjointed, discordant, and of course ineffectual," as Hamilton told General Pinckney, one measure that could be taken was the establishment of a serious party newspaper. Fenno had died in 1798 and the *Gazette of the United States* had, in effect, died with him. There were other Federalist journals of the same sort, but the election of 1800 had pretty well proved that vicious, personal journalism was no longer effective, if it had ever been. What was needed, Hamilton believed, was a paper that would follow a "line of temperate discussion and impartial regard to truth," while expressing Federalist criticism of the government and offering Federalist alternatives. Granting that "honest and virtuous men" were to be found in both parties, the paper would support the two-party system by presenting the Federalist case with unrelenting vigor but with a decent respect to the opinions of all citizens.

Hamilton set about founding such a paper almost as soon as he had settled back at home. He put up some money of his own and sought contributions, in the form of stock purchases, from his friends in business and finance. His campaign was successful, and on November 16, 1801, the first issue of the *New York Evening Post* appeared, a paper destined to live through numerous changes of ownership and editorial policy until today it is the only survivor of early American daily journalism.

The *Evening Post* was Hamilton's paper throughout the

rest of his life. The editor, William Coleman, was a devoted, even passionately enthusiastic Hamiltonian. His bias showed in everything he ever wrote. But he was neither vulgar nor invidious—at least customarily—and he raised the tone of political journalism in New York by several important notches. Hamilton himself acted as a kind of chairman of the editorial board—a one-member board!

Normally Hamilton did not himself write editorials for the *Evening Post,* and most of his articles were contributed to other papers or published as pamphlets. The *Post* nevertheless was his voice in city and state politics, while in its weekly national edition, the *Herald,* he reached into every state to encourage the Federalist faithful. Coleman's editorials were models of Hamiltonian style and doctrine. He was so completely devoted to his chief that his work was a fully conscious replica of Hamilton's own work. However, on frequent occasions Coleman would call in the evening at Hamilton's home and go over political developments with him in order to decide just how the *Post* should handle them. Sometimes Hamilton dictated to Coleman a rough draft; but more often he would simply talk about the subject while the editor made notes. Then Coleman would go back to the office and write his piece. In any case, it was soon known everywhere that whatever the *Post* said was what Hamilton thought.

The tradition of personal journalism has never died out on the *New York Evening Post.* In the generations after Hamilton the *Post* has had a number of eminent owners and editors. William Cullen Bryant, editor of the paper for almost fifty years, was a liberal who supported Democratic candidates; but E. L. Godkin, who followed him, was a great conservative and a Republican. In the twentieth century the *Post* has generally expressed a liberal point of view, though always independent of party. Henry Villard and his more famous son, Oswald Garrison Villard, kept up the national influence of the paper. In midcentury Mrs. Dorothy Schiff, aided by distinguished columnists like Max Lerner, Murray Kempton and Joseph P. Lash, made the *Post* a colorful and energetic exponent of the "New Frontier" brand of liberalism led by Adlai E. Stevenson and John F. Kennedy. In spirit the *Post* has often been a Jeffersonian, not a Hamiltonian paper. But its crusading vigor and its personal quality have remained its chief mark, just as Hamilton left it.

III

The moderate tone of the *Evening Post,* unfortunately, did not bring an end to the bitterness or violence that separated the close partisans of Jefferson and Hamilton. In 1802, for example, when renegade Republican James Callender published his scandalous attack on President Jefferson, including the revelation of Jefferson's youthful indiscretion in making advances to the wife of a friend, Coleman reprinted the material in the *Post.* Hamilton, who had not been consulted, was infuriated. There was such complete identity between himself and the paper that everyone immediately supposed he approved of the publication, or had instigated it. He had done nothing of the kind and deeply regretted the whole incident. Indeed, by that time he had had enough experience of journalistic character-smirching and malicious revelation of private, improper affairs not to wish such misfortune even upon his worst enemy. In order to leave no doubt where he stood on the matter, Hamilton published a statement in the *Post* disassociating himself from the slanderous piece and announcing his objection to seeing discussed in the *Post,* or in any other paper, "all personalities, not immediately connected with public considerations."

While Hamilton was organizing the *Post* in the summer of 1801, his son Philip was becoming deeply and tragically involved in his father's politics. On July 4, one George Eacker, a rabid young Republican lawyer, had made a public oration partly in praise of Jefferson but largely in the form of a diatribe against Alexander Hamilton. His language was extreme and his charges libelous. Among other things he asserted that the former inspector general had advocated strengthening the national defenses not to fight France but to bring civil war against the Republicans. Some time later, young Hamilton and several of his friends came upon Eacker in a New York theater and made vituperative remarks about him with the intention of being overheard. They were. Eacker grabbed Hamilton by the collar and shouted, "I will not be insulted by a set of rascals." He denounced Philip and his friends as "blackguards," and worse. The next day Philip Hamilton challenged George Eacker to a duel. It was a rash and hot-blooded, and, as it turned out, a fatal act.

Young Hamilton had inherited or developed all the aristocratic pretenses and prejudices of his father as well as his good looks and charm. He considered a man like Eacker a kind of poisonous enemy of all the values he thought worth fighting for. To challenge Eacker was somehow to fight for them as well as for personal honor. Philip's uncle, John Church, undertook to mediate the dispute, in the hope that Eacker could be persuaded to withdraw a word or two of his offensive language. But Eacker continued to be incensed and insisted on going ahead with the duel. "The expressions I made use of towards Mr. Hamilton," he told Church, "were produced by his conduct . . . I thought them applicable then, *and I think so still.*"

The duel was fought, prophetically, at Weehawken, New Jersey. Eacker shot first and killed Hamilton. The latter either withheld his fire entirely or intentionally fired too late. Eacker and his party were of the opinion that their man had simply been more accurate. The Hamilton group maintained that their man had not fired at all but that his pistol had accidentally discharged as he fell forward, mortally wounded. The report in the *Post* contained this interesting language: Philip Hamilton, "aware that the origin of the controversy lay with him, and averse to shedding blood, decided to reserve his fire, receive that of his antagonist, and then discharge his pistol in the air." If it is possible to find here the touch of a proud and saddened parent, such a touch is surely forgivable. Alexander Hamilton did write privately to more than one friend of his unabated sorrow and despair. The world, he replied to Benjamin Rush's letter of condolence, was "full of folly, full of vice, full of danger, of least value in proportion as it is best known." His son was well out of it, he told himself and his friends.

In his remaining years Hamilton continued his criticism of the Jefferson administration and worked hard but unsuccessfully for Federalist control of New York. The spirited freshness had largely gone out of his political writings and speeches. Sometimes his habitual opposition even led him to contradicting his own hopes. When the Louisiana Purchase was announced, for example, he took the position that Jefferson had acquired too much territory too quickly—forgetting for the moment, apparently, that he had himself been prepared only a few years earlier to take the whole area by force of arms!

But his ineffectual performance in politics was more than counterbalanced by his distinction as a practicing lawyer. Chancellor Kent, a partisan witness no doubt, as all witnesses are, set down this sketch of Hamilton as a lawyer:

> For the last six years of his life he was arguing cases before me. I have been sensibly struck in a thousand instances, with his habitual reverence for truth, his candor, his ardent attachment to civil liberty, his indignation at oppression of every kind, his abhorrence of every semblance of fraud, his reverence for justice, and his sound legal principles drawn by a clear and logical deduction from the purest Christian ethics, and from the very foundations of all rational and practical jurisprudence.

To illustrate Kent's point, Hamilton's greatest moment in the courtroom came in a civil liberties case.

The Republicans, who had suffered prosecutions for libel under the Sedition Law in Adams' administration—and against the advice of Alexander Hamilton—turned on their oppressors after Jefferson came to power in 1801. The Sedition Law itself had lapsed, but they sought to impeach Supreme Court Justice Chase for his conduct in sedition cases, and brought a number of prosecutions against newspaper editors and others in state courts under common law. One of these editors was Harry Croswell, publisher of a small-town paper called the *Wasp*, whose chief sport was stinging Republicans. In 1802 Croswell was charged with "wickedly and seditiously disturbing the peace and tranquillity" of the state of New York because he reprinted a stale slander to the effect that Jefferson had paid the infamous Callender to call Washington and Adams names that would in later times have been unprintable. On July 2, 1802, Croswell was convicted in a tumultuous trial marked by the judge's ruling that the truth of a libel could not be adduced as a defense for making it.

The political implications of the Croswell case were so evident that Federalists everywhere took an interest in it and rallied to Croswell's defense. The plea was for a new trial on the ground that insufficient time had been allowed for the preparation of Croswell's defense. On this precedent there was danger that Federalist writers anywhere could be rushed off to jail for attacking Jefferson. But the legal significance of the case was of still greater importance. The Sedition Act, passed by a Federalist Congress, had specifically allowed the truth of an allegation to be cited in defense against a charge of libel. The Republicans had objected on the ground that the truth of an opinion critical of Federalist officials could never be demonstrated to the satisfaction of Federalist judges. In the Croswell case the Republican judge was consistent in rejecting the truth criterion. But the case was certainly not the same as those under the Sedition Act, since Croswell's allegations purported to be statements of fact and were therefore subject to proof or disproof.

It was the combination of these political and legal implications which led Hamilton to take up Croswell's case. He was not prepared to stand by while Republican prosecutors and judges sent Federalist editors to jail, nor was he prepared to admit the doctrine that the proof of libelous charges could not be cited in defense. As he saw it, both the integrity of the two-party system he had once opposed, but now believed in, and the civil liberties of ordinary citizens were at hazard. In a kind of grand turnabout, Hamilton the old revolutionist appeared in the place of the more familiar Hamilton, skeptic of democracy and friend of aristocracy.

If there had ever been doubt that Hamilton's ability as a lawyer and advocate was of the highest order, his address to the court at Albany, February 13, 1804, removed it. If he could never marshal ideas or express them so persuasively as Jefferson, his mastery of law and logic was certainly superior to his rival's. It is only necessary to compare Jefferson's frantic efforts to convict Aaron Burr of treason in 1807 with Hamilton's performance in the Croswell case to see that in the law, at least, Hamilton was the better man.

Hamilton divided the subject of his appeal into two parts:

> The first as to the truth—whether, under a general issue of not guilty, it ought to be given in evidence. The other, as to the power of the court—whether it has a right, exclusively, over the intent, or whether that and the law do not constitute one complicated fact, for the cognizance of the jury, under the direction of the judge.

His argument developed both the rational basis and the relevant cases for both contentions. The English common law, despite a few instances cited by the prosecution, had normally allowed the evidence of truth to be cited in defense against libel. Intent could never be sensibly divorced from act in determining the facts of a case. These fundamental points were argued on behalf of the freedom of the press, which Hamilton defined as follows:

> The liberty of the press consists in my idea, in publishing the truth, from good motives and for justifiable ends, though it reflects on the government, on magistrates, or individuals.

If such liberty be not allowed, he said, "it excludes the privilege of canvassing men, and our rulers":

> It is in vain to say, you may canvass measures. This is impossible without the right of looking to men. To say

that measures can be discussed, and that there shall be
no bearing on those who are the authors of those measures, cannot be done. The very end and reason of discussion would be destroyed. Of what consequence to show
its object? Why is it to be thus demonstrated, if not to
show, too, who is the author? It is essential to say, not
only that the measure is bad and deleterious, but to hold
up to the people who is the author, that, in this our free
and elective government, he may be removed from the
seat of power. If this be not to be done, then in vain will
the voice of the people be raised against the inroads of
tyranny.

If this sounds more like what Americans had learned to expect
from Jefferson or Madison than from Alexander Hamilton,
one reason is the characteristic contribution Hamilton made
to his own legend. No doubt his reputed railing that "the
people is a great beast" is apocryphal, but his denunciation of
democracy and his excited expressions of fear and alarm at
lawless mobs or delinquent taxpayers earned him his reputation as a reactionary and obscured his libertarian views.
Another reason, perhaps more instructive, is that Jefferson and
Madison did most of their best work for civil liberties when
they were in opposition to the government; and so did
Alexander Hamilton.

In his plea for Croswell, Hamilton argued like the libertarian he always was, setting aside for the moment the
authoritarian he also always was. Judges, whom he had looked
upon in Federalist days as the strongest pillars of stable
society and government, he now suggested might subvert civil
liberty by acting as agents of the Executive:

. . . let me ask whether it is right that a permanent body
of men, appointed by the executive, and, in some degree,
always connected with it, should exclusively have the
power of deciding on what shall constitute a libel on our
rulers, or that they shall share it, united with a changeable body of men chosen by the people . . . it cannot be

denied, that every body of men is, more or less, liable to
be influenced by the spirit of the existing administration;
that such a body may be liable to corruption, and that
they may be inclined to lean over towards party modes.

Hamilton hastened to except the present company:

No man can think more highly of our judges, and I may
say personally so of those who now preside, than myself.

But he nevertheless could not "forget what human nature is,
and how her history has taught us that permanent bodies may
be so corrupted." This, ironically enough, from the one-time
advocate of a Senate appointed for life!

In the end, Hamilton's politics, too, came into play. For it
was possible to unite an appeal for the admission of truth as
evidence with a tongue-in-cheek concern for the reputation of
Mr. Jefferson:

It is desirable that there should be judicial grounds to
send the case back again to a jury. For surely it is not an
immaterial thing that a high official character should be
capable of saying any thing against the father of this
country.

It is important to have it known to the men of our
country, to us all, whether it be true or false; it is important to the reputation of him against whom the charge is
made, that it should be examined. It will be a glorious
triumph for truth; it will be happy to give it a fair chance
of being brought forward; an opportunity, in case of
another course of things, to say that the truth stands a
chance of being the criterion of justice.

Finally he planted his barbed hook deep in the flesh of the
Republican prosecutors. They had cited a case in which Lord
Mansfield had disallowed the truth of a libel as evidence.
Hamilton now congratulated his opponents on their choice of
heroes:

I am, I confess, happy to hear that the freedom of the English is allowed; that a nation with king, lords, and commons, can be free. I do not mean to enter into comparisons between the freedom of the two countries. But the attorney-general has taken vast pains to celebrate Lord Mansfield's character. Never, till now, did I hear that his reputation was high in republican estimation; never, till now, did I consider him as a model for republican imitation. I do not mean, however, to detract from the fame of that truly great man, but only conceived his sentiments were not those fit for a republic. No man more truly reveres his exalted fame than myself; if he had his faults, he had his virtues; and I would not only tread lightly on his ashes, but drop a tear as I passed by. He, indeed, seems to have been the parent of the doctrines of the other side. Such, however, we trust, will be proved not to be the doctrines of the common law nor of this country, and that in proof of this, a new trial will be granted.

As Hamilton no doubt anticipated, the Republican judges were not to be persuaded either by his eloquence, his logic or his barbs, and the Croswell case was lost. Hamilton's point, however, was won. The New York legislature presently enacted a criminal-libel statute which both permitted the truth of an allegation to be admitted as evidence for the defense and made the intent of the words published a matter for the jury to decide. The New York statute, in turn, became a kind of model copied by many other state legislatures. Thus Alexander Hamilton's contribution to the civil liberties of Americans, though hardly so well known, is fairly comparable with the stand against the Alien and Sedition laws made by Jefferson and Madison, and not so readily subject to abuse as was the states' rights doctrine of the Kentucky and Virginia Resolutions.

V

The bitterness of the Federalists in defeat knew almost literally no bounds. Jefferson, it seemed to them, meant the certain destruction of everything they had sought to build, the triumph of evil over virtue. No measure to prevent such a calamity was too extreme. Timothy Pickering, for example, seriously proposed a dismemberment of the Union. He advocated the establishment of a Northern Confederacy which would somehow wall out the surge of democracy—and Negro influence!—that was coming up through Virginia to Washington and beyond. To Alexander Hamilton he proposed that a military force be organized, in case Jefferson should refuse to allow peaceable secession, with Hamilton at its head. Pickering's plan was endorsed by other Federalist leaders.

But Hamilton was both too practical and too patriotic to condone any act of treason. "Dismemberment of our empire," he wrote Theodore Sedgwick, "will be a clear sacrifice of great positive advantages without any counterbalancing good, administering no relief to our real disease, which is *democracy.*" On the contrary, in Hamilton's perspective, democracy "by a subdivision, will only be the more concentrated in each part, and consequently the more virulent." His own moderate approach to the problem was to put the Federalist party on a strong national base. Accordingly, in the winter of 1802, he made an abortive effort to establish a national organization, issuing a call for a conference of Federalist leaders in Washington. But his old followers, Pinckney, Bayard and others, were either unavailable or without energy for the effort.

While Hamilton's patriotism remained solid and his political approach constructive, the chasm between himself and other Federalist leaders grew until it became unbridgeable. In the end, the whole issue was concentrated on the New York gubernatorial election of 1804. Hamilton's candidate was John Lansing. When Governor Clinton withdrew in order to become Jefferson's running mate as candidate for Vice-President, Lansing's chances looked reasonably good. But Hamilton's fellow Federalists were looking beyond the New York election. A new flirtation with Aaron Burr was in the making.

This time the Federalists thought to capitalize on sympathy for Burr as a man of "sound principles" who had been discarded by the hypocritical Jefferson as a dangerous potential rival. If Burr could be elected Governor of New York, with Federalist support, he might be a logical successor to Jefferson in the Presidency, and the Federalists would ride back into power with him.

This was precisely the kind of politics of desperation and chicanery that Hamilton would never play. He saw that the success of the venture, which he thought possible, would mean not the victory of the Federalists but their final demise. Burr, he said, would use them for election purposes, but would form a third party and play them off against the Republicans. In the end the Federalists would be discarded. In any case, it was not a question of winning elections so much as educating the people in matters of principle and policy. Burr, Hamilton insisted, had no principles; and his policy was only to take power in any way he could. By sending Burr to Albany, no ground would be gained in the great effort to limit Jefferson's democratic influence and eventually replace it by conservative republicanism. "To my mind," he told Morris, "the elevation of Mr. Burr, by federal means, to the chief magistracy of the United States, will be the worst kind of political suicide."

Indeed, so strongly did Hamilton reject the idea of Burr as President that to prevent it was one of his leading motives in giving energetic support to the move for an amendment to combine the election of President and Vice-President, designating the candidates officially for each office. It was the ambiguity of the Constitution on this matter that had produced the deadlock of 1800. In the future, Hamilton believed, Burr might succeed in dislodging Jefferson by the expedient of seducing a few Federalist votes away from the Federalist candidate. This would frustrate the will of the people and make a mockery of the electoral system, as had almost happened previously. Hamilton, of course, well remembered his own efforts to use the system to defeat John Adams; but to defeat Burr, he now thought, was even more important than defeating Adams had been. The loophole must be closed. And so he exerted all the influence he still possessed among Federalist members of Congress to persuade them to join the Republicans in passing the proposed amendment. The extent of his influence cannot, of course, be accurately measured, but he certainly does deserve a portion of credit for the adoption (1804) of the XIIth Amendment.

When his last-ditch effort to persuade Rufus King to run as a Federalist candidate for governor failed in the spring of 1804, Hamilton devoted his energies to defeating Burr. He did not, of course, campaign for Chief Justice Morgan Lewis, the Republican candidate, though he privately advised Federalists to vote for him, but he wrote and spoke against Burr whenever occasion was offered—and sometimes gratuitously. At this stage it is probably safe to say that Hamilton's power in New York politics was negligible. The Jeffersonian tide would no doubt have swept Lewis into office over Burr had Hamilton not participated in the campaign at all.

Burr, too, was finished. He and Hamilton were both relegated to political inconsequence by the great surge of Republicanism that accompanied the successes of the adored Jefferson's first term. Hamilton, secure in his political principles and "consoled," as he would have said, by his religious beliefs and the affection of his family, could take defeat with better grace than did most Federalists. And he was happy in the new home—"The Grange"—he was building in the country outside New York. In any case, he continued to hate Republicanism a good deal more than he hated Republicans. Despite his frequent and acid denunciations of Jefferson and other political opponents, the contest remained in his mind always basically a matter of principle.

Not so with Aaron Burr. That brilliant, charming, unhappy and rather sinister man took his licking with an outward show of good sportsmanship that covered somewhat thinly an irremediable inner bitterness. He was in a vindictive mood when a letter by Charles Cooper in an Albany paper, the *Register,* was brought to his attention. According to the letter, General Hamilton had said to the company at a dinner party that he "looked upon Mr. Burr to be a dangerous man, and one who ought not to be trusted with the reins of government." This, of course, was precisely the opinion of President

Jefferson and the reason he had dumped Burr, but the Cooper letter added a vague innuendo. Hamilton, Cooper said, had expressed "a still more despicable opinion of Burr." Nothing was specified and readers, including Aaron Burr, were left to infer what they liked.

Thomas Jefferson, the principal cause of Burr's downfall, was out of reach in the White House. But General Hamilton, his long-time enemy, was in New York, a private citizen, and a tempting target for revenge. What had Hamilton said at the notorious dinner party that was "still more despicable"? Burr would find out and demand an apology. If the apology were forthcoming, he would at least have the satisfaction of humiliating his opponent. If Hamilton refused to comply, a duel was a possible resolution to the overwrought state of Burr's emotions.

VI

And so it came about that on June 18, 1804, Aaron Burr, Vice-President of the United States, wrote a fateful letter to Major General Alexander Hamilton, ret., lawyer of New York City, his comrade in the Revolution a quarter of a century before, but afterward his political enemy for many years. Burr demanded satisfaction. "You must perceive, sir, the necessity of a prompt, unqualified acknowledgement or denial of the use of any expressions which would warrant the assertions of Dr. Cooper."

Hamilton saw no such necessity. If Burr did not dispute his right to the language actually quoted by Cooper, it was not reasonable for him to object to other political judgments that might be "still more despicable." Hamilton was "ready to avow or disavow, promptly and explicitly any precise or definite opinion" he might be charged with having stated, but Burr was asking him, instead, to disavow anything he might have said without specifying what it was. "I deem it inadmissible on principle," Hamilton told Burr, "to consent to be interrogated as to the justness of the inferences which may be drawn by others from what I may have said of a political opponent in the course of fifteen years' competition." He hoped and trusted that Burr would see the matter "in the same light," but if not, Hamilton would "abide the consequences."

Burr's reply was certainly calculated to bring the matter to the field of honor. "I regret to find in [Hamilton's letter] nothing of that sincerity and delicacy you profess to value." His honor, Burr repeated, had been impugned and "political opposition can never absolve gentlemen from the necessity of a rigid adherence to the laws of honor and the rules of decorum." Hamilton, in turn, could not accept Burr's language. "By your last letter, received this day, containing expressions indecorous and improper, you have increased the difficulties to explanation. . . ." After that, though Hamilton made several more attempts to avoid it, it was only a matter for the seconds to arrange the time and place of a duel.

The place chosen was Weehawken, New Jersey, where only three years before, Philip Hamilton had died from the bullet of a friend of Burr's. The date set was July 11. Hamilton had only a few days to make his will, set his affairs in order, and prepare his family for the possibility of his death. This was a good deal more than a possibility, as they all well knew, since Hamilton's principles were so strongly opposed to dueling that he was certain to "reserve" his fire. And Burr was known to be an excellent shot.

During the interval, Hamilton took time to set down an account of his "motives in meeting Burr." His reasons for trying to avoid a duel he listed as (1) his "religious and moral principles"; (2) the value of his life to his wife and children; (3) his sense of obligation to his creditors; and (4) that he was "conscious of no ill will to Col. Burr, distinct from political opposition." Burr's "manner of proceeding," however, had produced "intrinsic difficulties" which made it impossible to avoid the issue. These difficulties were: (1) Hamilton could not and would not apologize for political opinions, yet it was these which seemed to have given offense; (2) it was simply not "proper for him to submit to be questioned"; (3) Burr "appeared to . . . assume, in the first instance, a tone unnecessarily peremptory and menacing, and, in the second, positively offensive." On the other hand, Hamilton thought he had gone as far as he could to avoid a duel, perhaps even "further in the attempt to accommodate than a punctilious delicacy will justify." He left no doubt that though what he had said about Burr had never been said "on light grounds nor from unworthy inducements," he well understood that Burr might in all sincerity think himself inexcusably offended. "It is not my design, by what I have said," he wrote, "to affix any odium on the conduct of Col. Burr in this case."

Finally, Hamilton set down his intention to "reserve his fire."

> As well, because it is possible that I may have injured Col. Burr, however convinced myself that my opinions and declarations have been well-founded, as from my general principles and temper in relation to similar affairs, I have resolved, if our interview is conducted in the usual manner, and it pleases God to give me the opportunity, to reserve and throw away my first fire, and I have thoughts even of reserving my second fire, and thus giving a double opportunity to Col. Burr to pause and reflect.

There is no reason whatever to doubt the sincerity of this last-minute document. But as there are two sides—or more—in every serious disagreement or political issue, so from Burr's point of view the point of the forthcoming duel was rather different. To the Vice-President it seemed that Hamilton had repeatedly evaded the direct question Burr had raised. If, as Hamilton said, he would only respond to specific allegations and not to general statements that he had defamed Burr, then it seemed clear to Burr that there must indeed have been specific instances. Further, Burr knew as well as anyone else in New York that Alexander Hamilton was possessed of a free and caustic tongue. In short, there was no valid doubt that Hamilton had traduced Burr's reputation not once but often over the years. It is a moot question whether the matter ought to have been overlooked because it was involved in political antagonism, as Hamilton believed, or allowed to assume personal significance, as Burr saw it. What is certain is that from Burr's point of view Hamilton's behavior was at first deliberately offensive and then hypocritical, while Hamilton saw in Burr's pressing for apology a calculated effort to bring him to the field of honor. Both men were at least partly right. And so nothing could be settled by the duel itself. Tragedy was to be compounded by futility.

The whole matter was a remarkably well kept secret until the duel actually took place. On the fourth of July, for example, Burr and Hamilton met and participated in the celebrations of the Society of the Cincinnati. On that occasion Hamilton is said to have been greatly animated, even jumping on the table to lead the singing, while Burr watched the proceedings with his customary detachment. At home, a few days later, the Vice President wrote a letter to his son-in-law: "If it should be my lot to fall . . . yet I shall live in you and your son. I commit to you all that is most dear to me—my reputation and my daughter."

The two men met on the morning of July 11. On the first shot, Hamilton fell mortally wounded and died at the home of William Bayard thirty-one hours later. He was forty-nine years old, youngest to die of the Founding Fathers.

Van Ness, Burr's second, ever afterward maintained that Hamilton did not reserve his fire, but, on the contrary, fired first and at Burr. But his version was never acceptable. Burr's unpopularity and the shock of Hamilton's death guaranteed that the tragic scene would always remain obscured. Aaron Burr, though he could still attract a few ardent partisans, would never again reach the high ground of public favor and power he had once held; Alexander Hamilton, cast by events in the role of a martyr, gained in death the immense popular esteem he could never win in life.

New York City, and with it the whole nation, went into mourning. Hamilton was eulogized in papers that had never before had a kind word for him. His funeral, under the auspices of the Society of the Cincinnati, was the grandest and perhaps the most moving that had ever been held in the city. Burial was in Trinity Churchyard. Gouverneur Morris, after some curious soul-searching, spoke the eulogy. Near the grave the Cincinnati erected a tablet bearing this inscription, which has stirred the hearts of countless visitors ever since:

THIS TABLET
DOES NOT PROFESS TO PERPETUATE
THE MEMORY OF A MAN,
TO WHOM THE AGE HAS PRODUCED
NO SUPERIOR;
NOR TO EMBLAZON WORTH,
EMINENTLY CONSPICUOUS IN EVERY FEATURE
OF HIS COUNTRY'S GREATNESS;
NOR TO ANTICIPATE POSTERITY IN THEIR
JUDGMENT OF THE LOSS WHICH SHE HAS
SUSTAINED BY HIS PREMATURE DEATH;
BUT TO ATTEST
IN THE SIMPLICITY OF GRIEF,
THE VENERATION AND ANGUISH WHICH FILL
THE HEARTS OF THE MEMBERS OF THE
NEW YORK STATE SOCIETY OF
CINCINNATI
ON EVERY RECOLLECTION
OF THEIR ILLUSTRIOUS BROTHER,
MAJOR-GENERAL
ALEXANDER HAMILTON.

Chapter 7

THE MIND OF ALEXANDER HAMILTON

I

It has not been the custom of scholars and critics to include Alexander Hamilton among "great American thinkers." Historians of ideas, like Vernon Louis Parrington, noticed him chiefly because he was a coauthor of *The Federalist* and "villain" in Parrington's drama. He was included in the American Writers Series as a foil to Jefferson. But until recent years, little serious attention was given to his intellectual achievement. Indeed, until the revival of conservatism after World War II, in which Hamilton has become a preeminent figure, he was almost never classed as an intellectual man at all. This was a shallow judgment. By comparison with learned men like George Mason, Jefferson, Madison or the Adamses, no doubt Hamilton would not fully qualify. But in the age before mass communication, easy transportation and convenient shortcuts to knowledge, many public men had some intellectual pretensions, Hamilton more than most. Before the *Reader's Digest* or *Time* and *Newsweek,* before the *Britannica* and the *Americana,* before movie shorts and radio and television "educational programs," men of affairs read books, good and solid books, and often enough they meditated on what they had read and formed opinions. It is no exaggeration to say that the men of the American founding generation were better read and typically more thoughtful than any generation of their successors has been.

Intellectual statesmen, on the other hand, have not been common in the American tradition. Cabinet officers like William H. Seward, Charles Francis Adams, John Hay or

Elihu Root have appeared hardly more frequently than Presidents like Jefferson, Madison, the Adamses, Theodore Roosevelt, Wilson or Kennedy. The distinction is between the well-read man, of whom there have been many in American public life, and the man whose life is lived significantly in the mind, of whom there have been few. Among those few Alexander Hamilton holds authentic credentials of membership. If his theory of revolution was characteristic of his age, rather than original, if his conservative political philosophy was neither so profound as Burke's nor so learned as John Adams', his writings on both subjects were nonetheless sufficiently trenchant and articulate not only to have been widely read in their own time, as they were, but to deserve attention in this day, when constitutional democracy, whether liberal or conservative, is under steady attack by Marxists and near-Marxists. And Hamilton's work would be useful for Americans concerned with understanding the nature of their government, its potentials and its limitations, if there were no outside attacks at all. It is perhaps not too much to say, in fact, that the American spirit and attitude have never been fully American except when the Jeffersonian democratic tradition has been effectively challenged or countered by Hamilton's aristocratic republicanism.

II

An anecdote recorded by Jefferson has often been cited to point the contrast between the two men.

> The room [Jefferson's] being hung around with a collection of portraits of remarkable men, among them were those of Bacon, Newton, and Locke, Hamilton asked who they were. I told him they were my trinity of the three greatest men the world had ever produced, naming them. He paused for some time: "the greatest man," said he, "that ever lived, was Julius Caesar."

Jefferson, as we noted earlier, went on to say that Hamilton was "honest as a man, but, as a politician, believing in the necessity of either force or corruption to govern men." This encounter, though it emerges out of the biased recollections of an old man, is nevertheless instructive. Seen in the context of Hamilton's thought and character, it suggests a good deal more than Jefferson supposed it did. If rejecting Bacon, Newton and Locke in favor of Caesar indicates at a quick glance a kind of anti-intellectual obscurantism, a second consideration reminds us that while Jefferson's trinity was supremely the men of the modern era who proclaimed the efficacy of reason to solve the problems of man and nature, Caesar was supremely the man of all ages who doubted the efficacy of reason and advocated the use of force and "corruption" to maintain public order. One then remembers that though Hamilton never could accept the Federalist willingness to break up the Union in order to circumvent the triumph of democracy, he did repeatedly call for military measures against "mobs," and he did entertain, at least briefly, the idea of a military dictatorship for the same purpose. Finally, as one comes to know Alexander Hamilton, it is hard to avoid the notion that he was not only making a point but also pulling Jefferson's leg! No doubt Jefferson exaggerated his admiration for his trinity in order to prick Hamilton a bit, but Hamilton was perhaps quicker than Jefferson thought he was—and brought up a whole army to rout the three!

At any rate, Jefferson's thumbnail sketch of Hamilton is accurate. He was personally honest and he did believe that force or corruption or both were necessary to govern men. His view of human nature was pessimistic, in a vorldly rather than a Calvinistic sense. An Anglican in religic n, he believed that individual men were responsible for their actions and could to some degree shape their destinies. But if the characters of men were not predetermined by an angry God, they were nevertheless largely conditioned by nature to place self-interest above all other values, to be greedy and undisciplined, and inclined, in society, to be lawless rather than orderly. He rejected Hobbes's insistence that since life "in a state of nature" is "nasty, brutish, and short," without law or meaning, life in society requires dictatorship; but he agreed with Hume, his favorite philosopher, that statesmen should "govern men by their passions, and . . . animate them with a spirit of avarice and industry, art and luxury." In the Constitutional Convention, Madison noted that Hamilton appealed to Hume to justify "corruption" as "an essential part of the weight which maintained the equilibrium of the British Constitution." This was not to say that reason is an illusion or that people are never governed by it, but only that rational behavior is uncommon and not to be anticipated either by a wise man in his dealings with others or by a wise statesman in his dealings with affairs.

In his youth Hamilton's views were more sanguine. In his pamphlet battle with Samuel Seabury he relied heavily on Locke, and much of *The Farmer Refuted* reads like the work of George Mason or Jefferson himself. For example,

> . . . the origin of all government, justly established, must be a voluntary compact between the rulers and the ruled, and must be liable to such limitations as are necessary for the security of the *absolute rights* of the latter; for what original title can any man, or set of men, have to govern others, except their own consent? To usurp dominion over a people in their own despite, or to grasp at a more extensive power than they are willing to intrust, is to violate that law of nature which gives every man a right to his personal liberty, and can therefore confer no obligations to obedience.

A few years later, he told Gouverneur Morris that he approved the Articles of Confederation because of their reliance upon popular sovereignty, though he feared that the executive would be too weak. And once the Philadelphia Convention had produced the draft of the Constitution, Hamilton argued for its adoption both in *The Federalist* and in the New York State Convention on the ground that the great central power proposed would rest squarely on the will of the people.

But his experience in the war, where he saw self-interest prevail over patriotism to the point of mutiny, and such later public disturbances as Shays' Rebellion, had persuaded him by 1787 that popular government was not in fact to be trusted. In the supposed secrecy of the convention chamber at Philadelphia, he expressed the conviction that had replaced his earlier enthusiasm for "the people."

> All communities divide themselves into the few and the many. The first are the rich and well-born, the other the mass of the people. The voice of the people has been said to be the voice of God; and, however generally this maxim has been quoted and believed, it is not true in fact. The people are turbulent and changing; they seldom judge or determine right. Give, therefore, to the first class a distinct, permanent share in the government. They will check the unsteadiness of the second, and, as they cannot receive any advantage by a change, they therefore will ever maintain good government. Can a democratic assembly, who annually resolve in the mass of the people, be supposed steadily to pursue the public good? Nothing but a permanent body can check the imprudence of democracy. Their turbulent and uncontrolling disposition requires checks.

This was the view he ever afterward privately maintained, though in public he was always careful to pay lip service to the popular principle in the Constitution, and in *The Federalist* he gave effective support to it. There is, in short, a fundamental irony in Hamilton's public career: the best efforts of his mind and the whole energy of his body were devoted for years to making "work" a system in which he had little faith.

Clinton Rossiter, in his brilliant endeavor to show that Hamilton was more moderate than he had always seemed,* cites a passage written about 1795 in which Hamilton sounds more like Locke or Jefferson than Hume:

> The true politician . . . takes human nature (and human society its aggregate) as he finds it, a compound of good and ill qualities, of good and ill tendencies,

---

* *Alexander Hamilton and the Constitution* (New York: Harcourt, Brace, and World, 1964).

endued with powers and actuated by passions and pro-
pensities which blend enjoyment with suffering and make
the causes of welfare the causes of misfortune.

With this view of human nature he will not attempt to
warp or disturb its natural direction, he will not attempt
to promote its happiness by means to which it is not
suited, he will favor all those institutions and plans which
tend to make men happy according to their natural bent,
which multiply the sources of individual enjoyment and
increase national resources and strength, taking care to
infuse in each case all the ingredients which can be
devised as preventives or correctives of the evil which is
the concomitant of temporal blessing.

It is not necessary to question the sincerity of such sentiments
coming from Hamilton. Indeed, one could hardly expect him,
as a public man, to say anything else. The point, of course, is
that he constructed his system and based his own political
conduct on the "ill tendencies" he found in human nature, not
on the good. Sincerely doubting that an experiment in popular
government could be justified in terms of the nature of man,
he was nevertheless prepared to fight for it.

There were two strong reasons why he could live and work
under so burdensome an intellectual handicap. One reason was
patriotism. His prime motive as a soldier of the Revolution
had been the patriotic desire for independence, much more
than any wish to transform society. Once the war was won, it
was feeling for the nation that moved him to act against the
special interests of his own state, both in the legislature and in
the Congress. And it was his conception of a nation growing
out of the Union of the states which enabled him to accept
and work for a system of governing that Union which he considered a poor second best.

A second compelling reason for accommodating himself to
the irony of his public position was his belief in the liberty of
the individual human being, simply because he was a human
being. If experience and his reading of history taught him that
most men were mean and irrational much of the time, his

religious convictions taught him that there was a moral law, a law of God, superior to all men, good or bad, and that every man ought to be free to live as close to accord with that transcendent law as he could. The republican experiment at least made political and civil liberty possible. And so he agreed to the Bill of Rights, opposed in principle the Alien and Sedition laws, rejected the unpatriotic plans of his colleagues when Federalism seemed doomed and, in the end, as a lawyer spoke out for civil liberty as effectively as any man has ever done.

III

Hamilton's dark view of human nature made him a natural enemy of "natural religion," deism, indeed of the whole contemporary movement of "enlightenment" that so excited the imagination and intellect of Thomas Jefferson. Hamilton wrote no treatises on religion or ethics, kept no journal or commonplace book in which his sentiments on such matters were recorded. But occasionally he turned to them in the course of his political articles in a way to display not only what he vehemently opposed, but what he himself believed.

His unfinished piece on the French Revolution, for example, contains passages that show Hamilton's orthodoxy in religion and ethics and his conviction that the security of society depended on faith in established tradition and prescription. "Opinions," he wrote, "have for a long time been gradually gaining ground, which threaten the foundations of religion, morality, and society." Such opinions he traced to the substitution of "natural religion" for the "Christian revelation."

The Gospel was to be discarded as a gross imposture, but the being and attributes of God, the obligations of piety, even the doctrine of a future state of rewards and punishments, were to be retained and cherished.

Like Hume, whose *Dialogues Concerning Natural Religion* he probably knew, Hamilton saw that to undermine belief in the supernatural basis of religious behavior was to put too great a strain on reason and will, at least for most people. Unlike Hume, however, he was not at all persuaded by the critical analysis of revelation. Judging the argument against it by its consequences, Hamilton found his faith confirmed, not shaken.

The first consequence, as he saw it, was the questioning of the "very existence" of God. Once the denial was made, "the duty of piety [was] ridiculed, the perishable nature of man asserted, and his hopes bounded to the short span of his earthly state." At first, of course, such speculations were confined to the "conceited sophists" and the "haunts of wealthy riot." But in the end "irreligion . . . has more or less displayed its hideous front among all classes."

This second consequence produced, inevitably, the third and most serious:

> A league has at length been cemented between the apostles and disciples of irreligion and of anarchy. Religion and government have both been stigmatized as abuses; as unwarrantable restraints upon the freedom of man; as causes of the corruption of his nature, intrinsically good; as sources of an artificial and false morality which tyrannically robs him of the enjoyments for which his passions fit him, and as clogs upon his progress to the perfection for which he was destined.

This, to Alexander Hamilton, was the meaning of the French Revolution. If it was an inadequate view of the titanic upheaval that forced old Europe from the medieval into the modern era, it was nevertheless true as far as it went. French philosophers, from Rousseau to Condorcet, had said much the same things about religion, about human nature and about individual and social behavior. And the Revolution had in fact produced both the Terror and the "Feast of Reason."

Like Burke, Hamilton tied the violence and chaos of French Revolutionary society to the attack upon orthodox and traditional religion. Thus the French Revolution became in his eyes not only an object lesson of living history but the sign and symbol of all that was subversive of a stable, Christian society. Holding such views, it is not surprising that he came to see in Jefferson a kind of religious and political Satan figure, as in such a context he assuredly was. Jefferson had lived in France for years. He had been a member of the inner circle of advanced, liberal French thinkers and politicians. Among his close friends were Condorcet and La Rochefoucauld. At his dinner table these men, and others including Hamilton's friend Lafayette, had planned the first phase of the Revolution. Once the Bastille had fallen and his friends had come to power in France, Jefferson came home and immediately began to criticize and then to oppose all the measures Hamilton was taking to bring order and stability out of American chaos, to make sure that the French disaster was not repeated.

If Hamilton had actually watched Jefferson in action in France and listened to his conversations with the French radicals, American history might have been different. For he would have heard Jefferson counseling moderation at every turn, explaining that free institutions presume not only free men but men able to understand the responsibilities of self-government. Jefferson's constant theme was that republican success in America was owing not to political theory but to an educated citizenry. Most Frenchmen were illiterate; to ask them to undertake to build a viable republic without knowledge was utopian. Jefferson was no utopian. Perhaps Hamilton would have been most surprised had he heard the American Revolutionary enemy of Great Britain urging his French friends to imitate the British example! Keep your king, he advised them; only limit his powers by constitutional means. King, lords and commons will provide you with ample room to experiment and to respond to the needs of plain people while, at the same time, maintaining stable institutions of law and administration. As for the natural goodness of man, Jefferson argued that it was an illusion, a dangerous illusion. Man, as Locke had shown, was neither good nor bad innately. Progress was possible because man had the capability of learning; but progress would come only with hard work, with education; it was surely not inevitable. Perfection was a legitimate goal to strive for, but Jefferson had no faith it could be reached. He was a "meliorist," he said, not a perfectionist.

If Alexander Hamilton, set down in Paris in the 1780s, would not have said exactly these things, he would certainly have said much that was similar. Indeed, what he was saying to his fellow Americans was similar. He did not, of course, share Jefferson's skepticism in religion or faith in science. Hamilton was not a likely member of the American Philosophical Society. He did not admire Benjamin Franklin as a philosopher. Yet he numbered Rittenhouse and Rush among his friends, and took a lively interest in many kinds of experimentation. He even invited friends like C. C. Pinckney to send him seeds so that he could improve his garden, and read with interest and profit articles on agriculture.

But the similarities of thought and interest between the Virginian and the New Yorker were obscured from the first by their differences. And it was not long before Hamilton saw in Jefferson another Tom Paine under cover of a genteel manner. Just as Hamilton seemed to Jefferson a concealed but subversive monarchist, so Jefferson seemed to Hamilton the very type of the intellectual Jacobin. Thus each saw the other as he was not, by seeing only the extreme edges of his thought and purpose. Measured by his own ethical orthodoxy, Hamilton could only condemn Jefferson's utilitarianism. He preferred, at any cost, to stand for Christian virtue and the ancient code of honor. Because he was less able to command his passions than his code demanded, he sometimes fell into what he thought of as the paths of sin. When he did so, he made no excuses and suffered profound remorse. By contrast, Jefferson seemed to him a sanctimonious hypocrite. But in the end it was Jefferson's acknowledgment of humane principles that led Hamilton to intervene on his behalf in the election of 1800. Aaron Burr, Hamilton believed, was damned; Thomas Jefferson, for all his visionary ideas and offensive self-righteousness, might still be saved.

IV

To save Jefferson's soul was one thing; to save the Union of the American states was quite another. And Jefferson's democracy, in Hamilton's view, was the single most dangerous threat to that Union. The trouble with democracy, as he had concluded from his reading of political philosophers like Aristotle, Machiavelli, Hume and Montesquieu, from his study of the history of republican experiments, and as he thought he saw it in the rebellious outbursts in America, was that it flattered the people's weaknesses. Instead of teaching self-discipline, democracy seemed to say to everyone that he was entitled to his indulgences. If by nature man was unruly and appetitive, Hamilton could see no logic in presuming to build a stable society on the basis of the unrestrained popular will. The fact was that Jefferson could not see it either and was, in his own way, as anxious to prescribe limits as was Hamilton. Between the two men there were, of course, very great differences, but they nevertheless shared with most of their colleagues one major premise.

That premise was the virtue of property-holding and the sanctity of contract that accompanied ownership. Locke had established the modern trinity of "life, liberty, and property," and neither Hamilton nor Jefferson was prepared to argue that any one of these could be enjoyed without the others. It was ownership, in the received opinion of the day, which gave a man that sense of responsibility without which freedom would be license and which encouraged him to stand for stability and order in society. Jefferson was so confident of the intrinsic virtue of ownership that he suggested that the propertyless citizens of Virginia be granted land out of the public domain in order to qualify them for the franchise. Hamilton would have stopped short before that point.

If owning property was a natural right, and Hamilton believed it was, the virtues of property lay in the effort to acquire it as much as in the mere possession. The right was to acquire and hold property, not to have it conferred upon a man simply because he was a man. This was the premise of the entire Hamiltonian system, beginning with the securing of the public credit. In the *First Report* Hamilton frankly stressed the need to attach the men of property to the national government. "It cannot but merit particular attention," he wrote, "that among ourselves the most enlightened friends of good government are those whose expectations are the highest."

The funding system was devised "to justify and preserve their confidence." And it was these men, above all, whose investments would make possible the future industrial society, outlined in the *Report on Manufactures,* not the small farmers or the urban masses!

The appetitive instinct, in Hamilton's scheme, was to be channeled into constructive application of law and administration by securing the enjoyment of property. If it was natural to desire property and to strive to acquire it, it was natural also to wish to hold it in security. A government that promised security would command the loyalty of property-owners; in turn these men of property would place their power and their influence at the disposal of the government. Thus they would "establish public order on the basis of an upright and liberal policy."

But the stability thus achieved would have to be institutionalized. Because property-holding was unequal, there would always be the danger of popular risings against the rich, instigated by demagogues. As Hamilton told the Constitutional Convention, "nothing like an equality of property existed; that an inequality would exist as long as liberty existed, and that it would unavoidably result from that very liberty itself." So far from equality, Hamilton anticipated an increase of the "disparity . . . already great among us." Contrary to what he rightly foresaw as the modern tendency toward the equalization of property, he wished to protect that disparity and the means of increasing it. This was not, as has often been asserted by his critics, simply or even primarily because of his admiration for the very rich, like Philip Schuyler or Gouverneur Morris, but because he believed that only gifted individuals could bring about a permanent increase in the wealth of a nation. Government ought to serve such people because it was in the national interest to do so. "It will procure to every class of the community some important advantages, and remove some no less important disadvantages." In short, the rich and the well-born (the descendants of the rich) were a permanent force for stability and growth. Their role in society ought to be institutionalized at the very center of government.

Before and during the Philadelphia convention, Hamilton

argued for some adaptation of the British model for institutionalizing the power and influence of wealth. Specifically, he advocated an executive and an upper legislative house to serve "during good behavior." He afterward asserted that he had never proposed that these offices be held for life, which was certainly a good deal of a quibble. Hamilton's famous and presumably secret speech ever afterward plagued his political career, and he can perhaps be forgiven for insisting that he had not spoken quite so extremely as had been supposed. But if by "during good behavior" he did mean to leave the way open for impeachment of corrupt or treasonous officials, he surely intended equally that "good" officials should serve for life.

On his philosophical premises it could not have been otherwise. The claim of the men of property to essential control of the government could not be left dependent on so volatile a base as free elections. It was enough that the government should also include a popularly chosen legislative body to reflect the will of the people in all its variety and contrariety. And Hamilton was certainly sincere in his support of the House of Representatives. The turbulence represented by the House would be a useful safety valve at the worst; at the best, as the expression of the people's will it could guide and even check the administration. But the administration must remain the vital center of the government, just as the national government itself, checked in some degree by the states, must remain the vital center of the nation.

Did his belief in the desirability of life tenure for the President and the Senate, as well as the judges, mean that Hamilton was a monarchist? In the heat of party battles the Republicans certainly thought so. And in some sense it was so. If monarchy could be defined as a system in which the administrative powers are concentrated in one man and that man appointed for life and advised chiefly by a legislative body also serving for life, while the popular will is subordinated to the central, fixed power, then Hamilton was indeed a monarchist. But this was a matter of theory only. The plan was defeated at the Convention and never afterward seriously advanced.

In the heat of party rivalry Hamilton was frequently accused of something quite different from merely holding monarchical political principles. The point his enemies wished to make was that he advocated and worked for the subversion of the American republic and the substitution of "King, Lords, and Commons," not only on the British model but under British influence. There was exactly the same measure of truth in this charge as there was in the charge that Thomas Jefferson wished to introduce anarchy under the dominion of France—namely, none whatever.

While some of Hamilton's friends, like Gouverneur Morris, always thought of him as a "monarchist," and said so privately, they meant his philosophy, not his politics. His own view of the matter is well set forth in a fine letter to his friend—and Jefferson's—Colonel Edward Carrington of Virginia, at a time when the party battles were getting under way. He begins with a reference to the growing party split on the issue. The charge that there existed a "monarchical party meditating the destruction of State and republican government" was "absurd." "I assure you, on my private faith and honor as a man, there is not, in my judgment, a shadow of foundation for it." It was possible, he confessed, that "a very small number of men" might "entertain theories less republican than Mr. Jefferson and Mr. Madison," but he was persuaded, he said, that "there is not a man among them who would not regard as both criminal and visionary any attempt to subvert the republican system of the country." This was in 1792, and no doubt Hamilton's statement of the case was correct at that time. In later years there were profound changes of mind among the high Federalists. Pickering, for example, was prepared to break up the Union; Otis and Sedgwick were willing to subvert the electoral system. The Essex Junto had certainly given up on the republican system after the election of 1800. But, as the record shows, Hamilton himself never went to these extremes.

In his letter to Carrington he went on to set forth his political philosophy:

As to my own political creed, I give it to you with the utmost sincerity. I am affectionately attached to the republican theory. I desire above all things to see the equality of political rights, exclusive of all hereditary distinction, firmly established by a practical demonstration of its being consistent with the order and happiness of society. As to the State governments, the prevailing bias of my judgment is that if they can be circumscribed within bounds, consistent with the preservation of the national government, they will prove useful and salutary . . . As to any combination to prostrate the State governments, I disavow and deny it.

He expressed some concern with regard to potential conflicts between state and federal courts and suggested a Constitutional amendment to clarify the matter. "Otherwise," he said, "I am for maintaining things as they are; though I doubt much the possibility of it, from a tendency in the nature of things towards the preponderancy of state governments." It is worth observing here that while Jefferson's zeal for individual liberty blinded him to the probable consequences of emphasis on state as against national government, Hamilton's zeal for the national prerogative, on the other hand, enabled him to foresee correctly what those consequences would be. Anyone who follows the activities of the Governor and legislature of Alabama, for example, in their efforts in the 1960s to frustrate the national determination to end discrimination in education, or considers the awkwardness and inefficiency of dealing with the Eastern metropolitan area by means of seven different state governments, must conclude that Hamilton was sometimes more astute than Jefferson.

Not only did Hamilton fear the consequences of the rival power of state governments, he had some other doubts about republicanism. Again, he expressed his feelings frankly to Carrington:

I said that I was affectionately attached to the republican theory. This is the real language of my heart which I open to you in the sincerity of friendship; and I add that I have strong hopes of the success of that theory; but, in candor, I ought also to add that I am far from being without doubts. I consider its success as yet a problem. It is yet to be determined by experience whether it be consistent with that stability and order in government which are essential to public strength and private security and happiness.

This statement is certainly a key to Hamilton's political thought. It would be safe, perhaps, to say that in moods of optimism, when his political influence was ascendant, Hamilton was a fairly sanguine republican; in moods of despair, when his influence was diminishing, his doubts overcame his hopes. In the end he thought he saw anarchy and disorder triumphant. But even then he took pains to clear his reputation of any taint of subversive monarchism. For that purpose he was willing to go to the extreme of appealing to old George Clinton, his earliest and most consistent political enemy; and Clinton promptly replied, for publication, that to charge Hamilton with such political crimes was "odious and disreputable."

To focus, finally, on the "monarchism" v. "Jacobinism" issue through Hamilton's lenses, a passage from a speech he made in the election campaign of 1801 is a fair sample:

. . . the contest between us is indeed a war of principles —a war between tyranny and liberty, but not between monarchy and republicanism. It is a contest between the tyranny of Jacobinism, which confounds and levels everything, and the mild reign of rational liberty, which rests on the basis of an efficient and well-balanced government, and through the medium of stable laws shelters and protects the life, the reputation, the civil and religious rights of every member of the community.

Jefferson himself could not have phrased the matter more felicitously. "The mild reign of rational liberty" was precisely what he was always seeking. It is idle to regret that the two passionate partisans could not agree on what they meant by such language. Had they done so, their times would no doubt have been less turbulent, and there would have been, at the least, a different two-party system in the United States—and the nation might well have been the poorer.

V

That Hamilton's view of government was ultimately a moral one is to be expected from a man whose religious and ethical convictions were both orthodox and deeply held. Not only Hamilton, but most Americans, in fact, have tended to invoke moral imperatives—often moralistic—as an element of political rhetoric. Hamilton, had he been simply an exponent of American political pieties, would have no special claim to attention. But in one respect, at least, his moral approach to constitutionalism was both novel in its own time and interesting in later times. This was the line of demarcation he set to his own doctrine of implied powers.

Jefferson, as we saw in Chapter III, profoundly feared the acceptance of a rule of implication in construing the Constitution. He, and with him undoubtedly a majority of Americans, saw in the sanction of implied powers an open road to a new autocracy which might well be worse than the British. Their insistence on strict construction was not merely stuffy and reactionary, nor was it pettish; it was plainly moral. So, paradoxically, was Alexander Hamilton's plea for loose construction. The difference was that while the Jeffersonians saw government as a potential instrument for immoral action, Hamilton, like Aristotle, thought of government as itself the prime moral agent. In this he was a classicist. Whether his view was directly influenced by Aristotle, it is impossible to say. But he was certainly familiar with the *Politics* as a part of the corpus of political philosophy he read both as a young student and later on when he was preparing himself for a role in the Constitutional Convention.

At any rate, Hamilton's conviction that the state is a moral agent squares with the Aristotelian projection of ethics from the behavior of the individual to the behavior of the state, which he called politics. Just as right or virtuous action by the individual leads to happiness, which is the good for man, so right or virtuous action by the state leads to the good for society. Thus social happiness, "the good society," does not arise from the *absence* of government ("that government is best which governs least") but from the *presence* of government. The problem, therefore, is to build and maintain a virtuous government.

It is in this context that Hamilton's theory of implied powers in the Constitution is to be understood:

> That every power vested in a government is in its nature *sovereign*, and includes, by *force* of the *term*, a right to employ all *means* requisite and fairly applicable to the attainment of the *ends* of such power, and which are not precluded by restrictions and exceptions specified in the Constitution, or not immoral, or not contrary to the *essential ends* of political society.

Just as the good citizen, according to Aristotle, is both able to rule and willing to be obedient, so, according to Hamilton, government under the Constitution would rule only in obedience to the prescribed limits and the higher moral laws. Jefferson saw in the practice of implying powers a precedent for twisting the meaning of the Constitution so that government could quite literally do anything it wished. This was because he began with the assumption that government was an obstacle, not an instrument, to the good life. Hamilton, to the contrary, proposed to imply powers wherever they were essential, or even useful, to carry out the moral purposes of government. The limits he accepted would, for example, permit the establishment of a national bank, but not the subversion of the people's will, as expressed in elections, or of republicanism itself.

This was the crux not only of Hamilton's political theory but of his differences from most other American politicians of the time. The Republicans misunderstood him as advocating a government so strong, so much without limits, as to foster a tyranny; the Federalists broke with him when they became so set upon power as to be willing to use the government for what Hamilton considered an immoral purpose.

And it was this moral conviction of Hamilton's which entitles him to be called a conservative in political philosophy, not merely a reactionary. On any showing, it is Hamilton among all the Federalists from whom later Americans could continue to learn—not Ames, not Otis or Sedgwick or Cabot; not even Adams, learned though he was. Hamilton's politics continue to be relevant to his country because they are a politics of institution-building rather than of the simple struggle for power. And whether, in the nation's perennial oscillation, it is Jefferson's values or Hamilton's which enjoy the greater emphasis and popularity, Hamilton's insistence on the moral agency of government remains a necessary ideal for a republican democracy that continues to be experimental.

VI

In the end, Alexander Hamilton must be judged more by what he did than by what he said. One reason for this is highly positive—his deeds, in sum, constitute the largest contribution made by any one man to the building of the United States. Two other reasons for resting his fame upon actions rather than his writings are quite simple: he was not a scholar, and he often wrote in such haste and in such a passion of the moment that what he wrote was not worthy of a great writer.

But when these things are said, all has not yet been said. From Hamilton's writings—the addresses he made to the New York legislature in the 1780s, his speeches to the Constitutional Convention and the New York Ratifying Convention, from *The Federalist,* from his reports as Secretary of the Treasury and from his opinions on constitutional questions as a member of the Cabinet, and from his letters to many correspondents over many years—from all these can be extracted both a philosophical statement of political conservatism unmatched for its articulateness and its continuing relevance, and a system of governmental administration not equaled in scope or practicality by the work of any other American.

The vision of Thomas Jefferson proved the more attractive both to his own country and to the world, and it is no fair measure of Alexander Hamilton to compare his influence with Jefferson's. He was not that kind of man. He inspired only a

[174]

few intimates, not a whole people or even, over the long pull, a political party. From the first, his character frustrated the acceptance of his politics. His intellectual pride often verged upon arrogance, and few American statesmen ever suffered fools less gladly. But the trenchancy of his ideas forced their acceptance upon politicians who otherwise resented his superior airs. And the effectiveness of the institutions he built made certain that they would long outlive the political party he founded. He was not a great political philosopher nor a great writer, but his command of political philosophy and his facile and vigorous literary style were well suited to the needs of the great public administrator that he was.

BIBLIOGRAPHICAL NOTE

The Papers of Alexander Hamilton are being edited by Harold C. Syrett and Jacob E. Cooke and published by the Columbia University Press. The first nine volumes had been issued when this book was in preparation (1966). The Columbia edition will include all, or almost all, of the known writings of Hamilton and becomes the standard edition of his work as the volumes appear. For Hamilton's writings not yet published in the new edition, the best source is Henry Cabot Lodge's *The Works of Alexander Hamilton*, 12 vols., 1904, known as the "Federal Edition." Earlier editions are numerous, of which the best is that by Hamilton's grandson J. C. Hamilton. Hamilton's legal papers are being published in a separate edition, also by the Columbia University Press, under the editorship of Julius Goebel, Jr. The first volume appeared in 1964.

While older biographies are sometimes useful, and often more readable than the more recent ones, so much new information has come to light that it is unwise to rely entirely on any of them. Those by Lodge (1909) and F. S. Oliver (1915) are perhaps the best. Lodge's is especially sympathetic. So also is the swift-moving book by Nathan Schachner, *Alexander Hamilton*, 1946. Schachner also has done excellent, often entertainingly opinionated, studies of Jefferson, Burr, and of the Founding Fathers as a group, all of which are helpful in the study of Hamilton. Claude Bowers' heavily Jeffersonian volume, *Jefferson and Hamilton*, 1925, is a good counter to the pro-Hamilton books. Of two recent scholarly biographies, that by Broadus Mitchell (1957), though in two large volumes, is neither so well written nor so reliable as that by John C. Miller (1959). It is safe to consider Miller the principal authority.

The older studies of Hamilton's career and political ideas were usually written to serve a political purpose and are interesting more for what they reveal about the politics of their time than for what they say about Hamilton. The student who wishes to make a serious study of Hamilton's contributions to the origin and growth of the United States will find two more recent books particularly useful. Leonard White's *The Federalists,* 1948, the first in his four-volume administrative history of the United States, is a classic study of the building of the American national government. Hamilton is the hero, though the author's own views were decidedly more Jeffersonian than Hamiltonian. There is a rich abundance of detailed information and important statistics, but White never loses sight of the larger whole, and writes in a straightforward style often happily embellished by instructive anecdotes. Clinton Rossiter's *Alexander Hamilton and the Constitution,* 1964, is an exciting essay on the birth and growth of the Constitution. If it does not entirely succeed in its mission to make Alexander Hamilton acceptable to the modern liberal temper of the country he did so much to found, Rossiter's book does place him in a better perspective and rightly emphasizes what he did well rather than what he ought not to have done at all.

Julian Boyd's startling thesis, in *Number 7,* that Hamilton was in secret conspiracy with a British agent has been noted in Chapter IV. While Boyd's discoveries must of course be taken seriously, they need not necessarily be taken as seriously as he does.

Richard B. Morris has edited a large and well-selected collection of Hamilton's writings in one volume, *The Basic Ideas of Alexander Hamilton,* a Washington Square Press paperback (also published in a hard-cover edition as *Alexander Hamilton and the Founding of the Nation,* 1957), while Margaret Hall's *The Alexander Hamilton Reader,* 1957, is a useful paperback anthology of writings by and about Hamilton. Another useful paperback is Jacob E. Cooke's *The Reports of Alexander Hamilton,* 1964. Editions of *The Federalist* are numerous. That by Clinton Rossiter, a Mentor paperback, is introduced by a graceful and discerning essay.

Finally, students who wish to examine the ideas of Hamilton's principal opponents will find useful Joseph Charles's *Origins of the American Party System* (1963) and the present author's *The First Republicans* (1954) and *Jefferson* (Washington Square Press, 1963).

INDEX

Adams, Charles Francis, 156
Adams, John, 1, 30-31, 135, 149, 157, 174; his view of Presidential powers, 50; as Vice-Presidential candidate, 48; and Presidential election of 1792, 81-83 *passim;* elected President, 109-12; as President, 112-33 *passim*
Adams, John Quincy, 110
Adet, 111
Agriculture, Hamilton's views on, 72-73; Jefferson's views on, 72-73
Alexander Hamilton and the Constitution, 160n
Alexander Hamilton's Secret Attempts to Control American Foreign Policy, Number 7, 85n
Alien and Sedition laws, 26, 124, 126, 129, 130, 147, 162; *see also* Sedition Law
American Revolution, 4
American Revolution, The, 34n
Ames, Fisher, 62, 64, 102, 104, 174
"An American" (Hamilton pseudonym), 90
André, John, 17-18
Arnold, Benedict, 17-18
Articles of Confederation, 32, 36, 159; revision of, 23, 27, 33

Bache, Benjamin Franklin, 96
Bank of New York, 30

Bank of the United States, 13, 24, 26, 99; disputed in Congress, 60-68
Bayard, James A., 134, 135, 136, 148
Bayard, William, 154
Beckley, John, 115-18
Beckwith, George, 84-85, 86-87; his views on political situation quoted, 83-84
Benson, Egbert, 32
Bill of Rights, 162
Boorstin, Daniel, 34n
Boston Tea Party, 4
Boyd, Julian, 85n
Brown, Stuart Gerry, 35n
Bryant, William Cullen, 139
Burke, Edmund, 157, 163
Burr, Aaron, 6, 81-82, 98, 119, 124-25, 137, 144, 165; and Presidential election of 1796, 112; and Presidential election of 1800, 130, 133; and New York gubernatorial election of 1804, 149-51; his duel with Hamilton, 151-54

Cabot, George, 174
Callender, James, 116, 140, 143
"Camillus" (Hamilton pseudonym), 103
Carrington, Edward, 169, 170
Chase, Samuel, 142-43
Church, Angelica Schuyler (sister-in-law), 16
Church, John, 141
Clingman, Jacob, 92, 117-18

Clinton, George, 7, 31, 45, 48-49, 73, 81, 98, 148, 171
Clinton, Sir Henry, 17, 18
Coleman, William, 139
Condorcet, Marie Jean Antoine Nicolas Caritat, 163, 164
Constitutional Convention, Hamilton's speech to, 38-42; in Philadelphia, 37-42, 167, 168; in New York, 45-46
Continental Congress, Hamilton's criticism of, 8-9, 11-12
Cooper, Charles, 150-51
Cornwallis, Sir William, 22
Cotesworth, Charles, 113
Coxe, Tench, 36
Croswell, Harry, 143-47
Cruger, Nicholas, 2, 3

Daily Advertiser, 48-49
Dana, Francis, 9-10
Declaration of Independence, 102
Debt, funding of the, 53-58, 60, 71; Federal assumption of the, 56-60
Dialogues Concerning Natural Religion, 162
Dorchester, Lord Guy Carleton, 84, 86
Duane, James, 11
Duer, William, 44, 71, 79-80
Du Pont, Pierre Samuel de Nemours, 123

Eacker, George, 140-41
Ellsworth, Oliver, 126, 128
Essex Junto, 169
Ethics, 35n

Farmer Refuted, The, 159
Federalist, The, 42-45, 52, 106, 156, 159, 160, 174
Federal Reserve Board, 2
Fenno, John, 69, 96, 138
First Report on the Public Credit, 53-54, 166-67

First Republicans, The, 35n
Ford Motor Company, 71
Franklin, Benjamin, 25, 38, 165
French Revolution, Hamilton's views of, 162-65
Freneau, Philip, 69, 80
Fries' Rebellion, 128-29
Funding the debt, *see* Debt

Gallatin, Albert, 76, 93, 95, 101, 105-06, 106
Gates, Horatio, 7, 9
Gazette of the United States, 51, 69, 138
Genêt, Edmond, 89-91
Genius of American Politics, The, 34n
Gerry, Elbridge, 42; sent to France, 115, 120
Giles, William, 91, 101
Godkin, E. L., 139
Gordon, William, 9-10
Grant, Ulysses S., 51
Grenville, Lord William, 101

Hamilton, Betsy (wife), 14-17, 52, 119
Hamilton, James (father), 2
Hamilton, Philip (son), 23, 140-41
Hamilton, Rachel (mother), 2
Hammond, George, 87, 100
Hartz, Louis, 34n
Hay, John, 156
"Helvidius" (Madison pseudonym), 91
Henry, Patrick, 126
History of the United States for the Year 1796, The, 116
Hume, David, 159, 160, 162-63, 166
"Hurricane letter," 3

Independent Journal, 43
Industrial economy, Hamilton's views on, 73-78

Jackson, Andrew, 65
Jameson, Franklin, 34n
Jay, John, 44, 47, 87, 110, 117, 130; sent to England, 87, 94-95; his treaty, 99-106, 113
Jay Treaty, 99-106, 113
Jefferson and the Rights of Man, 35n
Jefferson, Thomas, 1, 16, 26-27, 42, 50, 114-15, 156, 157; compared with Hamilton, 1-2, 4-5, 34-35, 157-74 *passim;* compared with Schuyler, 16; his views on the American Revolution, 34; attacks Society of the Cincinnati, 35; as Secretary of State, 59-60, 64; his views on national bank, 64, 66; his views on agriculture, 72-73; and Presidential election of 1792, 80-83 *passim;* criticized by Beckwith, 83-84; his foreign policy, 83-91 *passim;* and Presidential election of 1796, 109; elected Vice-President, 109-12; and Jay Treaty, 100-03; and Presidential election of 1800, 130; elected President, 129, 133-36; as President, 137-51 *passim*

Kempton, Murray, 139
Kennedy, John F., 1, 51, 110, 140, 157
Kent, James, 142
King, Rufus, 38, 47, 126, 127; and New York gubernatorial election of 1804, 150
Knox, Henry, 7, 122, 124
Knox, Hugh, 3

Lafayette, Marie Joseph, 7, 18, 19, 21, 164
Lansing, John, 38; and New York gubernatorial election of 1804, 148

Lash, Joseph P., 139
Laurens, John, 8, 14
Lavien, Rachel Fawcett, *see* Hamilton, Rachel
Lee, Charles, 21
Lerner, Max, 139
Lewis, Morgan, 32; and New York gubernatorial election of 1804, 149-51
Liberal Tradition in America, The, 34n
Lincoln, Abraham, 50, 110, 112
Livingston, Brockholst, 32
Livingston, Edward, 101, 104
Locke, John, 159, 160, 164
Louisiana Purchase, 142

McHenry, James, 112, 113, 120, 122, 124, 125, 127, 128; dismissed, 132
McNamara, Robert, 71
Machiavelli, Niccolò, 166
Madison, James, 1, 11, 19, 26-27, 90-91, 94, 102, 105-06, 107, 109, 145, 156, 157, 159, 169; compared with Schuyler, 16; works with Hamilton, 24-28, 33, 37; at Constitutional Convention, 38-40 *passim;* and *The Federalist,* 44-45; securing Washington's election, 47; his views on national bank, 62-63; in 1st Congress, 56-60 *passim;* in 2nd Congress, 60-68 *passim;* and Presidential election of 1792, 80-83 *passim;* considered for mission to France, 114-15
Malone, Dumas, 35n
Mansfield, Lord William Murray, 146-147
Marshall, John, 6; sent to France, 115, 120
Mason, George, 42, 156, 159
Monroe, James, 19, 36, 94-95, 113; and Hamilton-Reynolds

affair, 92-93, 116-19; sent to France, 95

Montesquieu, Charles Louis, 166

Murray, William Vans, 126

Morris, Robert, 13, 24-28, 33, 37, 41, 52, 65, 87, 134, 135, 138, 154-55, 159, 167, 169

Muhlenberg, John, and Hamilton-Reynolds affair, 92-93, 116-18

National Gazette, The, 69, 80, 82

Navigation Acts, 86, 103

New York Commercial Advertiser, 123

New York Evening Post, 138-40

"No Jacobin" (Hamilton pseudonym), 90, 91

Opinion on the Constitutionality of the Bank, 66

Otis, Harrison Gray, 102, 125, 169, 174

"Pacificus" (Hamilton pseudonym), 90

Paine, Tom, 5, 110-11, 165

Parrington, Vernon Louis, 156

Paterson, William, 79

"Phocion" (Hamilton pseudonym), 31, 32

Pinckney, Charles Cotesworth, 113, 120, 122, 124, 138, 165; sent to France, 113, 115; and Presidential election of 1800, 131, 133

Pinckney, Thomas, 131, 148; and Presidential election of 1796, 110-12

Pickering, Timothy, 112, 113, 114, 116, 124, 132, 148, 169; dismissed, 132

Pitt, William, 57

Polk, James, 50, 67

Presidential elections, of 1796, 109-12; of 1800, 129-36; of 1804, 148-51

Priestley, Joseph, 123

Pseudonyms (Hamilton), see "An American"; "Camillus"; "Helvidius"; "No Jacobin"; "Pacificus"; "Phocion"; "Publius"

"Publius" (Hamilton pseudonym), 43, 44

Randolph, Edmund, 19, 36, 64, 66, 91, 94; compared with Schuyler, 16; at the Constitutional Convention, 37-42 passim

Register, 150

Report on a National Bank, 60-61

Report on Manufactures, 73-78, 167

Reynolds, Maria, Hamilton's affair with, 16, 92-93, 115-19

Rittenhouse, David, 165

Rochambeau, Jean, 17, 22

Roosevelt, Franklin D., 1

Roosevelt, Theodore, 157

Root, Elihu, 157

Rossiter, Clinton, 34n, 160

Royal Danish American Gazette, 2-3

Rush, Benjamin, 141, 165

Rutgers v. Waddington, 31-33

Schiff, Dorothy, 139

Schlesinger, Arthur Jr., 34n

Schuyler, Elizabeth, see Hamilton, Betsy

Schuyler, Philip (father-in-law), 7, 13, 16, 49, 167; Hamilton's letter to, 19-21

Sedgwick, Theodore, 126, 134, 148, 169, 174

Seabury, Samuel, 4, 159

Sedition Law, 142-47; see also Alien and Sedition laws

Seedtime of the Republic, 34n
Seward, William H., 156
Shays, Daniel, 36-37
Shays' Rebellion, 159
Shippen, Peggy, 17-18
Smith, Adam, 75, 76
Smith, William, 105, 110
Society for Useful Manufactures (S.U.M.), 78-79
Society of the Cincinnati, 154; conflicting attitudes toward, 35
Stevenson, Adlai, 51, 110, 140

Talleyrand, Charles, 120; quoted, 1
Tammany Hall, 82
Tariff, Hamilton's views on, 73-78 *passim*
Taylor, John, 127
Taxes, to pay for war, 25; Hamilton's views on, 25-26
Troup, Robert, 23, 32
Treaty of Paris, 87, 94
Truman, Harry, 51

Van Cortlandt, Philip, 148
Venable, Abraham, and Hamilton-Reynolds affair, 92-93, 116-18
Venture, 17
Villard, Henry, 139
Villard, Oswald Garrison, 139

Vital Center, The, 34n
Volney, Constantin, 123
Vumenal, 22

Washington, George, 1, 28-30, 45, 104-05, 120-22, 124; first meeting with Hamilton, 6; friction over Benedict Arnold, 17-19; President of the Society of the Cincinnati, 35; his early association with Hamilton, 6-21 *passim;* elected President, 47-48; defining Presidential powers, 49-50; his social life, 50-52; and Presidential election of 1792, 80-83; criticized by Beckwith, 83-84; retires from the Presidency, 106-09; his farewell address, 107-08
Washington, Martha, 52
Wasp, 143
Wealth of Nations, The, 76
West Point, 122
Wilson, James, 38, 41, 65
Wilson, Woodrow, 110
Wolcott, Oliver, 64, 93, 98, 112, 122, 123, 124, 125, 132, 134, 157

XYZ Affair, 115, 120

Yates, Robert, 38, 48